TWO-OVER-

GAME FORCE:

AN INTRODUCTION

by
Steve Bruno
and
Max Hardy

Published by
Devyn Press, Inc.
Louisville, Kentucky

First Printing — September 1993
Second Printing — September 1994
Third Printing — September 1996
Fourth Printing — July 1999

Printed in the United States of America.

Published by
Devyn Press, Inc.
3600 Chamberlain Lane, Suite 230
Louisville, KY 40241
1-800-274-2221

ISBN No. 0-939460-01-7

<u>Dedication</u>

For my teacher and my friend — My Dad
— S.B.

For Richard Walsh — who taught me the System
— M.H.

TABLE OF CONTENTS

TABLE OF CONTENTS

INTRODUCTION

The Two-Over-One Game Force bidding system is the one used by most experts on the tournament circuit today. Its natural yet accurate style enables well-practiced as well as casual partnerships to achieve successful results.

Until now the books which attempted to teach the Two-Over-One system were rambling narratives aimed at the advanced practitioner. It was difficult for the beginning student to discern basic principles of the system.

Steve Bruno and Max Hardy have written the first true Two-Over-One textbook — one that clearly describes the principles which make the Two-Over-One system different from Standard methods. Their examples are meaningful and clear. The quizzes accurately summarize the contents of each chapter. The Tools & Gadgets section describes many of the enhancements available to the modern bidder.

I recommend Two-Over-One Game Force: An Introduction to any bridge player who is interested in learning this highly-successful bidding system.

Paul Soloway
Mill Creek, Washington
June 1992

FOREWORD

This book was written to teach bridge players who are comfortable with Standard methods of bidding how to use the Two-Over-One Game Force system of bidding.

Many books have been written about the Two-Over-One or "Walsh" or "Eastern Scientific" system of bidding. Unfortunately for the uninitiated, these books have usually been written in such a way as to make the reader have to "pick out" the fundamental tenets of the Two-Over-One system from pages of narrative that attempt to present the entire system rather than start by giving the basics.

As the system gained in popularity and became the one used by most tournament experts today, the need arose for a textbook - one that could be used by teachers or self-teachers.

This book is an attempt to provide that needed textbook. It is not an attempt to preach the superiority of the system or to praise the pet treatments or conventions of the authors.

If the reader becomes a happier bridge player by having easy access to the basics of the approach, the goal of the authors will have been achieved.

PART I

THE SYSTEM

CHAPTER 1

THE BASICS

I. WHAT IS TWO-OVER-ONE GAME FORCE?

"Two-over-one game force" is a system of bidding whose overriding principal is: **When responder bids a lower-ranking suit at the two level in response to his partner's opening bid of one in a suit, the partnership is committed to bid to a game contract or higher.** For example:

NORTH	EAST	SOUTH	WEST
1♠	Pass	2♣	

or

NORTH	EAST	SOUTH	WEST
1♥	Pass	2♦	

or

NORTH	EAST	SOUTH	WEST
1♠	2♣	2♦	

If responder bids a higher-ranking suit at the two level, over interference (other than One Notrump, Double or a cue-bid so that it is not a jump bid, the partnership is also committed to bid on to a game contract or higher. For Example:

NORTH	EAST	SOUTH	WEST
1♥	2♣	2♠	

At this stage of the auction we cannot be certain about what suit (if any) will be the trump suit or whether or not we may be interested in a slam-level contract. We can be sure that the partnership must continue bidding until a game level contract is reached. Therefore, responder (South in the auction above) must have game going values in order to bid Two Spades.

As anyone who is even slightly familiar with bidding systems knows, **there are exceptions.** But those exceptions do not change the basic philosophy of the system.

Two-over-one game force is a "natural" bidding system. Almost every bid expresses the values or length in the suit it <u>seems</u> to express. In other words, when we bid hearts, we usually have hearts; when we jump the bidding, we usually have more values than if we do not jump the bidding (a major exception is the preemptive jump shift response used by many). In this respect, two-over-one is very similar to Standard American or "Standard" bidding. As in Standard bidding, many conventions can be integrated into the system. These conventions add elements of artificiality to any natural bidding system. Some conventional bids do not show the values or the distribution they seem to indicate. All of these conventions are available to and used by Standard bidders as frequently as they are used by two-over-one bidders. Some conventions are more necessary or more beneficial because we are playing the two-over-one system. These conventions are just as usable by Standard bidders.

There are only two bids which have significantly different meanings in the context of the two-over-one system than they do in the context of Standard bidding: the <u>forcing notrump</u> and the "<u>two-over-one</u>" bid of a lower-ranking suit. These two bids are the cornerstones of the two-over-one system. Remember: **Responder can not bid two of a lower-ranking suit without game-forcing values.** The entire bidding system is based on that principle. Many of the conventional sequences have been constructed to "get around" the obstacles that exist to show length in a lower-ranking suit without making a "two-over-one" bid. The forcing notrump is the tool which makes invitational and non-forcing sequences possible. Otherwise, most bids in the two-over-one system are identical to the bids you would make using a Standard bidding system based upon five-card major suit opening bids.

Years ago the Kaplan-Sheinwold system, the Roth-Stone system, and other five-card major systems utilized the forcing notrump bid to find eight-card (4-4, 5-3 and 6-2) fits in suits which were lower-ranking than opener's first-bid suit. The two-over-one bid was not forcing to game. The determination to use two-over-one auctions to force to game was originated in the late 1960's by Richard Walsh, John Swanson, and Paul Soloway.

What is so innovative or appealing about the two-over-one system? Perhaps it is the fact that both partners often know "instantly" whether or not the partnership has values sufficient to justify adventuresome bidding. Although, as we shall see, there are more times than not when that information is not "sent" or "received" until later in the auction. Perhaps some of the appeal is in the use of the forcing notrump and the well-defined auctions that it facilitates, although the forcing notrump can be utilized with almost any bidding system. Perhaps some players enjoy the gamut of conventions which have become part of the "two-over-one" system — conventions such as *SLAM RELAYS, INVERTED MINORS, NEW MINOR FORCING* and *FOURTH SUIT FORCING.* Even though these conventions could be part of almost any system, they are perceived, especially by newer players, as instruments of the two-over-one system.

Whatever the reason, the two-over-one system is currently enjoying widespread popularity, and it has become mandatory for any player who wishes to be competitive in today's bridge world to understand it thoroughly.

II. THE REASONS TO PLAY TWO-OVER-ONE

One property of "standard" bidding which experienced players find objectionable is the undefined strength of many of its initial sequences, thus making the partnership unsure of its potential until late in the auction. This uncertainty causes severe consternation, particularly when the opponents enter the bidding, as in the following auction:

NORTH	EAST	SOUTH	WEST
1♥	Pass	2♣	2♦

With Example #1 should North bid Two Notrump, double, or pass? If the partnership is playing standard methods, North is afraid to do anything but pass because South may have a hand of limited strength (10 or 11 HCP) with extra-long clubs. Thus, a penalty double may be a losing action or a notrump bid may place the partnership too high. With such a hand, South was going to rebid Three Clubs or pass Two Notrump when it was his turn to bid. "He could still do that over Two Notrump or Double," you say? That's true. But should he? Would he? What if West had bid Three Diamonds rather than Two Diamonds? How much defensive strength could North count on from South? Does South hold Example #2, Example #3 or Example #4?

Example #1
- ♠ K42
- ♥ KQ1062
- ♦ Q964
- ♣ K

Example #2
- ♠ Q87
- ♥ J4
- ♦ 5
- ♣ AQJ10862

Example #3
- ♠ A76
- ♥ J5
- ♦ 3
- ♣ AQJ10852

Example #4
- ♠ A653
- ♥ A3
- ♦ K5
- ♣ QJ1082

Playing two-over-one, North would know South has the values to force to a game contract (Example #3 or #4) Therefore, there should be sufficient defensive tricks in the South hand to give North a choice of good bids with Example hand #1. And it's not only when a two-over-one is made that a player may have confidence in his partner's values. Although the auctions which start with a "one-over-one" sound and usually look remarkably like standard auctions, there are inferences available which give the opening bidder more information upon which to base his actions than are typically available in most "standard" partnerships. (See: WEAK JUMP SHIFTS, FUNNY JUMPS and SUPPORT DOUBLES).

Another important advantage to playing the two-over-one system is that it is not necessary to take up valuable room by jumping the bidding to show a good hand; therefore, exploration for strain or level can proceed easily. For example:

NORTH	EAST	SOUTH	WEST
1♦	Pass	2♣	Pass
2♦	Pass	3♦	

is an auction that in Standard methods would not even be forcing. But in the world of two-over-one this is definitely forcing and could be the start of a very strong sequence. Cue-bidding of a major suit can be accommodated at a level low enough that the partnership can easily decide whether to stop in a notrump game or to continue to bid toward a diamond or notrump slam. In other words, with a good hand, neither the opener nor the responder has the need to jump at his first opportunity in order to assure that the auction will not die prematurely, thereby saving valuable bidding space.

QUIZ # I

Within the context of the two-over-one system, are the following auctions forcing to game?

	NORTH	EAST	SOUTH
1.	1♠	Pass	2♣
2.	1♦	Pass	2♣
3.	1♦	Pass	2♥
4.	1♦	2♣	2♦
5.	1♠	2♣	2♥
6.	1♥	2♦	2♠
7.	1♥	Pass	2♥
8.	1♥	Double	2♦
9.	1♥	1NT	2♦
10.	1♣	2♣	2♦

Your partner opens with a bid of One Heart. Your right hand opponent (RHO) passes. Do you have sufficient values to force to game with the following hands?

11. ♠ A65
     ♥ Q432
     ♦ K974
     ♣ 106

12. ♠ A4
     ♥ Q86
     ♦ J98743
     ♣ AQ

13. ♠ AQ62
     ♥ J64
     ♦ KJ9
     ♣ Q96

14. ♠ A5
     ♥ 6
     ♦ KQJ108743
     ♣ 64

15. ♠ KQJ964
     ♥ 2
     ♦ A43
     ♣ KJ4

16. ♠ K63
     ♥ Q1086
     ♦ AQ943
     ♣ 6

ANSWERS TO QUIZ # I

1. Yes. This is a standard two-over-one game forcing auction.

2. Yes. Even though no major suit has been bid, the auction is still forcing to game.

3. No. This is a bid at the two level in a <u>higher</u>-ranking rather than a <u>lower</u>-ranking suit without interference. It is a "jump-shift." Many partnerships play jump-shifts show very strong hands, at least game forcing and probably slam invitational. But most two-over-one players use *WEAK JUMP SHIFTS,* which are discussed in the *TOOLS & GADGETS* section.

4. No. This is merely a simple raise of partner's suit. The two-level bid is not in a <u>new</u> suit.

5. Yes. Even though there is interference, the bid is forcing to game. Some partnerships play the two-over-one bid is "off in competition." But until we reach the discussion in the *TOOLS & GADGETS* section, we will play this auction forcing to game.

6. Yes. In competition, the two-level bid in a new suit (without a jump) is game forcing.

7. No. There is no new suit.

8. No. The system is off over an immediate takeout double.

9. No. The system is off over natural One Notrump overcalls. If South had enough values to force to a game contract, he would probably double the One Notrump bid for penalties.

10. No. If the Two Club bid is for takeout, then other bids are available to South to show a strong hand. For example, if

Two Clubs shows the major suits, then a bid of Two Hearts or Two Spades is available as a cue bid. Some partnerships play the Two Diamond bid here as game forcing. On the basis of frequency, it is better not to do so. This is an uncommon auction and falls outside the logical order of the two-over-one system. Don't let it distract you from comprehending the principals of the system.

11. No. We need 12 or 13 points opposite our partner's sound opening bid to force to game.

12. Yes. Two Diamonds is the correct response.

13. Yes. We have sufficient values. Although we have the strength to make a two-over-one bid, we do not have adequate length in any lower-ranking suit to bid diamonds or clubs. The correct bid is One Spade. Note that a bid of one-over-one does not guarantee **or deny** sufficient values to force to game. By making a bid of one-over-one we are delaying the announcement of our strength. We could have any number of high card points greater than five.

14. No. We would like to bid diamonds, but we do not have 12 or more points. We cannot force to game by bidding Two Diamonds. We must bid One Notrump. As we shall later see, this bid is forcing and we can later bid diamonds. Also later, we will learn we could immediately bid Three Diamonds if we were playing *INVITATIONAL JUMPS*.

15. Yes. See #13.

16. Yes. Although we do not have 12 or more high card points, we have sufficient values or "points" in support of hearts as trumps. We know that we will continue to bid until a contract of Four Hearts (or higher) is reached. Because we have the values to bid on to game, we are "permitted" to make a two-over-one bid of Two Diamonds. Splinter responses are discussed in the *TOOLS & GADGETS* sections.

CHAPTER 2

OPENING THE BIDDING

I. THE REQUIREMENTS FOR AN OPENING BID

The requirements to open the bidding in the two-over-one system are about the same as they are for most Standard bidding methods. Opener must have about 12 HCP and a convenient rebid. Partnership preferences and styles will dictate how far these requirements should be stretched. For our purposes, the 12 HCP standard shall be assumed. Example #5 is **not** an opening bid. Example #6 is strong enough to open the bidding.

Example #5
- ♠ Q10643
- ♥ J5
- ♦ A64
- ♣ A32

Example #6
- ♠ K10643
- ♥ J5
- ♦ A64
- ♣ A32

II. NOTRUMP

The two-over-one partnership can choose any range of one notrump opening bids it enjoys for integration into its bidding system; in other words, none of the two-over-one principles is affected by the range of one notrump opening bids. Most two-over-one partnerships use the range of 15 to 17 HCP for a one notrump opening bid. The "baby" notrump range of 10 to 12 HCP or the "weak" notrump range of 11 to 14 or 12 to 15 is also usable.

Two notrump opening bids are usually in the standard range (20 to 22 HCP).

III. STYLE

As in standard bidding, style affects almost all aspects of two-over-one bidding. If the partnership style is **aggressive,** then it will choose to open more 11-point hands than a partnership whose style is **conservative.** Similarly, the **aggressive** partnership will make a game-forcing bid (perhaps a two-over-one) with hands that a **conservative** partnership may characterize as merely invitational in strength. Example #7 is such a hand. In response to an opening bid of One Heart, the **aggressive** partnership's bid would be Two Diamonds. The **conservative** pair would start with a bid of One Notrump, and later make an invitational bid in Hearts. Or, perhaps, the conservative pair would make an immediate limit raise in hearts by bidding Three Hearts, or make a delayed game invitation by starting with one notrump and rebidding Three Hearts.

Example #7
♠ J3
♥ Q64
♦ A10962
♣ KJ6

It is up to each partnership to choose a style and attempt to produce bidding sequences that are consistent with that style.

IV. CHOOSING AN OPENING BID

Two-over-one is a "Five-card Major" system. That means that when you open the bidding with One Heart or One Spade, you are guaranteeing that you have at least five cards in the suit bid. This requirement applies to opening bids in first, second, third and fourth seats. However, many players prefer to occasionally open a four-card major in third or fourth seat. (See *DRURY*). But our discussions will assume a suit of at least five-card length. If your major suits are equal in length, and at least five cards long, you should start the auction with a bid of One Spade.

If you have no five-card major and you do not hold a hand of between 15 to 17 HCP with "balanced" distribution, but you have at least 12 HCP, you must open the bidding with a minor suit. But which one? As you might expect, if the length of the two suits is not identical, it is most common to open the bidding with a one bid in the longer suit. (Note: if you have four diamonds and five clubs and can not rebid notrump over either major suit response from partner and do not have adequate strength to make a reverse bid, you may elect to open the bidding with One Diamond. See Example #8.)

If the suits are of equal length, open the higher ranking — diamonds — unless both suits are of only three-card length, in which case open the bidding with One Club. See Examples #9 and #10. In each case, we would open the bidding with One Diamond. Some experts would recommend an opening bid of One Club with Example #9 because there is a strong preference for your partner to lead a club rather than a diamond if your partnership eventually defends. The correct opening bid is a matter of partnership preference and agreement.

Example #8
- ♠ AJ
- ♥ J4
- ♦ KQ43
- ♣ Q8732

Example #9
- ♠ A84
- ♥ KJ
- ♦ 9876
- ♣ AJ42

Example #10
- ♠ J7
- ♥ Q43
- ♦ AK42
- ♣ KJ94

Example #11
- ♠ KJ4
- ♥ Q1062
- ♦ AK4
- ♣ 962

Example #12
- ♠ Q42
- ♥ Q752
- ♦ KQ6
- ♣ KQ6

With Examples #11 and #12 we would open the bidding with One Club. The reason we choose to bid three-card clubs before three-card diamonds is that by bidding clubs, we give our partner an easy opportunity to bid diamonds or raise clubs with a weak hand, thus making our fit easier to find. Also, a bid of One Diamond tends to imply a distinct preference for diamonds, which is not the case when we are 3 -3. When the opening bid is One Diamond, partner can frequently expect a four-card holding.

QUIZ #II

Do the following hands have sufficient values to open the bidding?

1. ♠ KQ106
   ♥ J985
   ♦ AJ92
   ♣ 9

2. ♠ AQ6
   ♥ KJ9742
   ♦ J82
   ♣ 6

3. ♠ AKQJ10863
   ♥ J62
   ♦ 4
   ♣ 3

If you force to game opposite your partner's opening bid of One Spade with the following hands, is your action best characterized as "moderate" or "aggressive"?

4. ♠ 2
   ♥ KJ6
   ♦ Q10832
   ♣ AJ72

5. ♠ Q832
   ♥ 2
   ♦ AJ64
   ♣ KJ86

6. ♠ J
   ♥ K62
   ♦ AQJ974
   ♣ J83

What is the correct opening bid with each of the following hands?

7. ♠ AQ762
    ♥ K9832
    ♦ A4
    ♣ 3

8. ♠ Q4
    ♥ J63
    ♦ AQ42
    ♣ KJ63

9. ♠ K2
    ♥ 63
    ♦ AJ83
    ♣ KQ962

10. ♠ 2
    ♥ Q42
    ♦ KJ83
    ♣ AQJ82

11. ♠ KJ103
    ♥ Q42
    ♦ AQ2
    ♣ J63

12. ♠ KQ
    ♥ AJ
    ♦ J832
    ♣ K9632

ANSWERS TO QUIZ #II

1. No. There are only 11 HCP. Without more unusual distribution, we need 12 HCP to open the bidding.

2. Yes. Even though there are only 11 HCP, the extra-long rebiddable heart suit, coupled with the outside scattered values, makes our hand valuable both offensively and defensively.

3. No. We have 11 HCP and an extra-long and solid spade suit, but we have no outside, defensive values. If we open the bidding with One Spade and our left hand opponent (LHO) makes a bid of, say Five Diamonds, and our partner doubles, what should we do? Our partner expects some defensive tricks from us. Do we have any?

   Some experts would say our hand is too good to open with a pre-emptive bid. Since it would be imprudent to open with a One Spade bid, it is suggested that we pass or open with a bid of Four Spades. Partnerships which play the Namyats convention may have the option of opening this hand with a bid of Four Diamonds.

4. Aggressive. You have only 11 HCP and no spade fit.

5. Moderate. Even though you have only 11 HCP, your good fit with your partner's spade suit and your singleton enhance the value of your hand. A splinter bid is in order.

6. Aggressive. Even though you have 12 HCP, you have no fit with your partner and your values outside of your long suit are "soft." This is a hand you might not open in first or second seat and, therefore, may not want to commit to a game level contract.

7. One Spade. With equal length in your two long suits, you open with the higher-ranking.

8. One Diamond. When you do not have a five-card major and have to choose a minor suit as an opening bid, you choose the higher-ranking (diamonds) of equal-length suits when they are at least four cards in length.

9. One Diamond. Even though your clubs are longer, you must prepare for a rebid. Certainly, no matter which minor suit you open, you will rebid One Notrump over your partner's response of One Heart. How about a rebid over your partner's One Spade response? You should not rebid One Notrump because the opponents have been primed to lead a heart. If you open One Club and rebid Two Clubs, you lose the flexibility of being able to play in a 4-4 diamond fit, since, with four spades and four or five diamonds, responder must systemically bid One Spade over One Club with a hand which is not strong enough to force to game. The One Diamond opening allows you to rebid Two Clubs over your partner's One Spade bid, catering to playing the part-score in the minor suit which offers the best fit.

10. One Diamond. Once again, we would not rebid One Notrump over our partner's response of One Spade or One Heart. Thus, we start with a bid of One Diamond and follow with

a rebid of Two Clubs so we can get both of our suits mentioned and show an unbalanced hand.

11. One Club. When we have no five-card major and are 3-3 in the minors, we start with a bid of One Club.

12. One Club. This hand is different from #9 and #10 above because we <u>will</u> rebid One Notrump over our partner's response of One Spade or One Heart. So we might as well start the bidding with our longest suit; we don't have to distort the description of our hand in order to prepare for a rebid.

CHAPTER 3

RESPONDING TO OPENING BIDS OF ONE OF A MINOR

I. PRIORITIES

The aim of any bidding system is to reach the best contract. The scoring method which determines our results tells us that the most desirable strain is a major suit. Therefore, two-over-one, like standard bidding, is preoccupied with finding the "golden fit" — the eight-card major suit fit. With that in mind, let's look at the priorities of a responder to an opening bid of one of a minor.

1) Bid a major suit which is at least four cards long; seek the "golden fit" of eight cards;

2) Look for a notrump contract. Bid notrump if you have no four-card major and have all suits stopped and have flat distribution. Or bid a new minor suit in an attempt to reach a final contract in notrump;

3) Look for a playable minor suit contract by bidding the other minor or raising your partner's minor. Keep in mind that your partner may have opened a three-card minor suit. Therefore, you should have at least five cards in the suit to raise immediately.

These rules categorically apply to all hands of less than opening strength; hands which, opposite a minimum opening hand, would not be bid to the game level. The same rules, with one notable exception, also apply to hands of opening strength or better. We will discuss that exception later. The point is: Remember the priorities of the system. Let's look at possible responses for hands of different strengths.

II. RESPONSES WITH LESS THAN 6 HCP

With no long higher-ranking suit, pass.

With a six-card or longer higher-ranking suit, bid a weak jump shift. (See: *WEAK JUMP SHIFTS*)

III. RESPONSES WITH 6 TO 12 HCP

With one four-card major suit, bid it, regardless of the shape of the rest of your hand. In Example #13, responder would bid One Spade in response to an opening bid of One Club from partner. He may later find a convenient way to bid his longest suit.

With both four-card majors, bid One Heart. The spade suit will not be missed as we shall later see. If you respond One Spade with Example #14, the heart suit may be missed altogether.

With neither four-card major and a "balanced" hand, bid One Notrump with 6 to 10 HCP. A "balanced" hand is one with no voids and no singletons. Example #15 fits that description as does Example #16. The correct response to your partner's opening bid of One Diamond is One Notrump.

Example #13
- ♠ 10843
- ♥ Q2
- ♦ KJ9832
- ♣ Q

Example #14
- ♠ QJ43
- ♥ K982
- ♦ J42
- ♣ Q2

Example #15
- ♠ K83
- ♥ Q96
- ♦ J6
- ♣ J8432

Example #16
- ♠ Q62
- ♥ 104
- ♦ KQ82
- ♣ J764

28

With neither four-card major and an unbalanced hand, either a bid of One Diamond over an opening bid of One Club is appropriate or a raise to Two Clubs or an <u>Inverted</u> raise to Three Clubs (See INVERTED MINORS) would be correct. Since our opening bids in the minor suits may be in a three-card suit, we must be careful before raising the bidding in that minor suit. Therefore: **ALL IMMEDIATE RAISES TO OPENING BIDS OF ONE OF A MINOR GUARANTEE AT LEAST 5-CARD SUPPORT.**

This rule applies to hands of all strengths. When we raise One Club to Two Clubs (assuming we are NOT playing the Inverted Minor convention), we are telling our partner several characteristics of our hand. We are promising that:

1) We have 6 to 9 HCP.
2) We do not have a four-card major suit.
3) We do not have a balanced hand.
4) We have at least five cards in the club suit.

Double raises in the minors tell the same story, but for hands of the 10 to 12 HCP strength. Thus, when we make a <u>limit raise</u> from a bid of One Club to a bid of Three Clubs we are telling our partner:

1) We have 10 to 12 HCP.
2) We do not have a four-card major suit.
3) We do not have a balanced hand.
4) We have at least five cards in the club suit.

If we have an unbalanced hand with diamonds, we respond to an opening bid of One Club with a bid of One Diamond with hands of 6 HCP or greater.

If we have an unbalanced hand with clubs, our responses to opening bids of One Diamond differ, depending on our hand strength. For hands of 6 to 9 HCP, we respond with a bid of One

Notrump if we have no singletons. Example #17 is such a hand. If we have a singleton, we hope we can raise diamonds to the two level. Example #18 is one of those hands that can not be described scientifically. The recommended bid is One Notrump.

If our unbalanced hand with clubs is of the 10 to 12 HCP strength, we would respond with an invitational bid of Two Notrump if we had no singletons. An attractive alternative with Example #19 is an <u>invitational jump</u> to Three Clubs (See *INVITATIONAL JUMPS*) if the partnership is playing that convention. If you are not playing the convention, you should again bid an invitational Two Notrump. Under no circumstance can you bid Two Clubs in response to an opening bid of One Diamond without the values to force to game (12 HCP).

NOTE: A RESPONSE OF TWO IN A LOWER-RANKING SUIT CANNOT BE MADE WITHOUT GAME-FORCING VALUES.

Example #17

♠ 32
♥ K8
♦ Q62
♣ QJ9864

Example #18

♠ 3
♥ Q6
♦ J83
♣ A987632

Example #19

♠ Q6
♥ J43
♦ QJ
♣ AJ10843

IV. RESPONSES WITH MORE THAN 12 HCP

When you have game-going values opposite your partner's opening bid, you can afford the luxury of delaying your search for the "golden fit" in a major suit to explore a game or slam contract in a minor suit.

In other words: when you know you will eventually drive on to a game or slam contract, respond to your partner's opening bid of one of a minor in your longest suit — even if you must delay bidding your four-card major suit in order to bid your five-card or longer minor suit.

In Example #20, you would respond One Heart to your partner's opening bid of One Club. In Example #21, you would respond Two Clubs to your partner's opening bid of One Diamond. In Example #22, you would respond One Heart to your partner's opening bid of One Club. Although hearts is not your longest suit, it is your longest unbid suit. You will show club support later. If you have two suits - one major and one minor - of equal length, bid the major suit first (See Example #23. Bid One Spade in response to your partner's opening bid of One Diamond.)

If you have both majors of exactly four-card length, bid hearts first ("up the line"), as you would with any strength hand. (In Example #24, bid One Heart in response to your partner's opening bid of One Club).

If your majors are both five or six cards long, bid spades first, as you would with any strength hand. See Example #25.

V. CONTINUING THE AUCTION AFTER OPENER'S NOTRUMP REBID.

When your partner has rebid One Notrump or has jump rebid Two Notrump after your major suit response to his opening bid of one in a lower-ranking suit, your search for the "golden

Example #20
- ♠ K4
- ♥ Q10832
- ♦ A
- ♣ KQ743

Example #21
- ♠ 43
- ♥ AKJ4
- ♦ J8
- ♣ KJ843

Example #22
- ♠ J4
- ♥ J642
- ♦ AQ
- ♣ AJ632

Example #23
- ♠ J6432
- ♥ KQ
- ♦ J
- ♣ AK432

Example #24
- ♠ Q982
- ♥ J863
- ♦ A4
- ♣ KQJ

Example #25
- ♠ Q9863
- ♥ AJ642
- ♦ Q7
- ♣ K

fit" of eight cards in a major suit is not over. We have already seen that, with hands having less than game-invitational strength, we "sign off" by simply rebidding a long suit or by taking a preference:

Example #26
♠ 2
♥ A98754
♦ Q643
♣ 43

NORTH	EAST	SOUTH	WEST
1♣	Pass	1♥	Pass
1NT	Pass	2♥	

or

Example #27
♠ 42
♥ J985
♦ K2
♣ K9742

NORTH	EAST	SOUTH	WEST
1♣	Pass	1♥	Pass
1NT	Pass	2♣	

Typical hands are shown in Examples #26 and #27. Notice both hands have less than 11 HCP and are not well-suited to a notrump contract opposite a typical hand by partner.

Example #28
♠ Q10863
♥ J982
♦ K62
♣ 4

When responder holds at least five spades and at least four hearts and less than invitational values (6 to 9 HCP), he responds with a bid of One Spade to his partner's minor suit opening bid and then bids Two Hearts over opener's One Notrump rebid. The sequence is non-forcing. Example #28 shows responder's typical hand for such bidding.

Example #29
♠ 52
♥ KJ9732
♦ AQ4
♣ J4

With invitational values (10 to 12 HCP) and a six-card major suit, the correct method to invite partner to bid a game contract is by means of a jump rebid of your major suit.

NORTH	EAST	SOUTH	WEST
1♣	Pass	1♥	Pass
1NT	Pass	3♥	

See Example #29. Some partnerships play that the invitation can be accepted only in responder's suit. That is, opener has only two choices: to bid Four Hearts with a maximum (13 to 15 HCP) or to pass with a minimum (11 to 12 HCP). The theory is that, since the partnership has an 8 or 9 card major-suit fit, it is unwise to choose any other strain as a final contract. However, players who aspire to become successful match-point players may want to include Three Notrump as a possible final contract after the auction above.

Hands with invitational values and the 5-4 or the 4-5 major suit pattern are expressed by using the *NEW MINOR FORCING* convention, discussed in the **TOOLS & GADGETS** section.

Invitational hands which are 5-5 or 6-5 in the major suits are described by jumping to Three Hearts over opener's One Notrump rebid. The auction of:

NORTH	EAST	SOUTH	WEST
1♣	Pass	1♠	Pass
1NT	Pass	3♥	

shows Example #30. The Three Heart bid is invitational to Three Notrump, Four Spades or Four Hearts. If opener takes a preference to Three Spades, responder should pass.

Example #30
♠ Q10865
♥ KJ942
♦ A4
♣ 3

Some partnerships play this sequence as forcing to a game-level contract and use the *NEW MINOR FORCING* convention to show the invitational hand with five spades and four or five hearts. Once again, the "correct" bid is a matter of partnership agreement and preference.

The *NEW MINOR FORCING* convention (NMF) is used to discover eight-card major suit fits that are not uncovered during the first round of bidding. In uncontested auctions such as:

NORTH	EAST	SOUTH	WEST
1♥	Pass	1♠	Pass
1NT			

or

NORTH	EAST	SOUTH	WEST
1♦	Pass	1♠	Pass
1NT			

or

NORTH	EAST	SOUTH	WEST
1♣	Pass	1♥	Pass
1NT			

it is possible that the partnership has an eight-card major-suit fit. In the first auction, the partnerships could have a 5-3 spade fit. Opener would be unlikely to raise his partner's spade suit immediately with only three-card support.

In the second auction, the partnership could have a 5-3 spade fit or a 4-4 heart fit. If responder has five spades and four hearts, he would have bid spades first. Opener would rebid One Notrump rather than "reverse" to Two Hearts if he held a hand in the range of strength of 11 to 15 HCP.

In the third auction, the partnership could have a 5-3 heart fit or a 4-4 spade fit could exist IF THE PARTNERSHIP AGREEMENT IS TO BYPASS A 4-CARD SPADE SUIT IN ORDER TO REBID ONE NOTRUMP WITH ALL BALANCED HANDS.

To facilitate this quest for the eight-card major suit fit, the *NEW MINOR FORCING* convention is employed. A complete discussion of this convention is found in the **TOOLS & GADGETS** section. But, at this time, it is necessary to describe how the *NEW MINOR FORCING* convention fits into our bidding scheme.

Hands of less than invitational strength cannot be cooperatively bid in such a way as to explore a hidden eight-card major suit fit. As discussed above, when responder has a weak hand that is not suited to a notrump contract, he must choose to rebid his five or six-card major or to make a "sign off" bid by taking a preference to a suit that is lower-ranking than his original suit.

If that lower-ranking suit is the only unbid minor suit, he cannot bid it at the two level because he will be activating the *NEW MINOR FORCING* convention. In other words, if the auction proceeds:

NORTH	EAST	SOUTH	WEST
1♦	Pass	1♥	Pass
1NT	Pass	2♣	

The Two Club bid is artificial, says nothing about the club suit, and propels the partnership to a level of bidding higher then is justified by responder's weak range (6 to 9 HCP).

So, how can we arrange to play in a minor suit that we know holds at least an eight-card fit for the partnership? Responder can make a non-forcing bid in an unbid minor suit by utilizing the *FUNNY JUMP* convention. The auction of:

NORTH	EAST	SOUTH	WEST
1♦	Pass	1♥	Pass
1NT	Pass	3♣	

shows at least a six-card club suit, no more than four hearts, and a weak hand (6 to 9 HCP). It is non-forcing. If responder has only

35

four or five cards in the unbid minor suit, he would not "take out" One Notrump, even with a singleton in an unbid suit. If he had a fifth heart and felt notrump was too risky, he could rebid his major suit at the two level. Example #31 is a hand that would utilize the auction above. (See *FUNNY JUMPS.*)

With Example #32, responder would rebid Two Hearts if he feared a notrump contract. He could not rebid Two Clubs because that bid activates the *NEW MINOR FORCING* convention and propels the partnership to heights not supported by responder's assets.

Once the *NEW MINOR FORCING* convention is employed, the partnership is committed to continue bidding until a contract of Two Notrump, Three of a Major or Four of a Minor is reached. Of course, there are exceptions. See *NEW MINOR FORCING* to learn more about those exceptions.

Example #31
♠ 4
♥ K842
♦ Q2
♣ Q108632

Example #32
♠ 4
♥ K8642
♦ Q32
♣ Q1082

Example #33
♠ Q
♥ K842
♦ QJ963
♣ K62

Responder's hands with six-card suits and invitational values are discussed above; jump rebids of the long suit are appropriate. Hands with a five-card fit for opener's minor suit can be described by a jump to three of opener's minor suit over his One Notrump rebid. The auction of:

NORTH	EAST	SOUTH	WEST
1♦	Pass	1♥	Pass
1NT	Pass	3♦	

shows five or more diamonds and 9 to 11 HCP. See Example #33. Note that responder has only a four-card heart suit. The delayed jump support bid for opener suggests only four-card length in responder's first bid suit. Armed with the knowledge that responder has probably only four hearts, at least five diamonds and 9 to 11 HCP, opener should be able to make an intelligent choice on the next round of bidding.

Hands of invitational strength without a five-card major or without five-card support for opener's minor are generally described by raising One Notrump to Two Notrump. With a four-card major and five cards in the unbid minor suit and invitational values, responder could employ the *NEW MINOR FORCING* convention. But, without extensive practice and discussion, these hands are generally better served by simply raising One Notrump to Two Notrump.

The exploration for the eight-card major-suit fit with all hands having game-forcing values (12 or more HCP) is done by using the *NEW MINOR FORCING* convention. All hands which contain game-forcing values and a fit for opener's suit are described via the same convention. Since nearly all jumps are either non-forcing (*FUNNY JUMPS*) or invitational, employing the *NEW MINOR FORCING* convention is the only way we can proceed toward a game contract when we have sufficient values. Example #34 and Example #35 are responder's hands with which we want to proceed to a game-level contract and, to do so, we activate the *NEW MINOR FORCING* convention after the auction of:

Example #34
♠ 4
♥ KJ82
♦ KQ986
♣ A63

Example #35
♠ K2
♥ QJ9863
♦ A4
♣ K63

NORTH	EAST	SOUTH	WEST
1♦	Pass	1♥	Pass
1NT	Pass	?	

Two Clubs is the correct bid here. Opener responds as if we are seeking a three-card heart holding by him, or a four-card spade holding IF OUR PARTNERSHIP BYPASSES FOUR-CARD SPADE SUITS TO REBID ONE NOTRUMP. Appropriate rebids by opener are discussed in the *TOOLS & GADGETS* section. After opener's response to the Two Club bid, responder, with Example #34 will tell opener that he has a diamond fit with him; that, perhaps he was less interested in discovering an eight-card heart or spade fit than in starting a description of a hand with game-forcing values and a diamond fit.

With Example #35, responder had the option to jump to four hearts, but elected *NEW MINOR FORCING* since he had honor cards in all suits. If opener shows a doubleton heart, he has the option to play Three Notrump, but should play four hearts when the fit is nine cards.

The purpose of this cursory discussion of the uses of the *NEW MINOR FORCING* convention has been to demonstrate that hands of all strengths and all shapes can be described over opener's One Notrump rebid.

QUIZ #III:

Partner opens the bidding with One Club. What is our initial response with each of the following hands?

1) ♠ KQ3
    ♥ 104
    ♦ Q632
    ♣ J982

2) ♠ AK63
    ♥ 10432
    ♦ A43
    ♣ QJ

3) ♠ J632
    ♥ K9
    ♦ 5
    ♣ KQJ842

4) ♠ Q83
    ♥ 63
    ♦ A42
    ♣ Q9863

5) ♠ 932
    ♥ 4
    ♦ KJ984
    ♣ A962

6) ♠ J9
    ♥ A43
    ♦ KQ4
    ♣ J9832

Partner opens the bidding with One Diamond. We respond One Heart and he rebids One Notrump. What is our next bid with each of the following hands?

7) ♠ 6
    ♥ K983
    ♦ Q432
    ♣ K983

8) ♠ 8
    ♥ QJ984
    ♦ K32
    ♣ Q832

9) ♠ Q43
    ♥ Q983
    ♦ A42
    ♣ K83

10) ♠ J83
    ♥ KJ942
    ♦ Q62
    ♣ A8

11) ♠ J73
    ♥ KQJ82
    ♦ A4
    ♣ KJ2

12) ♠ Q4
    ♥ Q98762
    ♦ J43
    ♣ QJ

13) ♠ J6
    ♥ Q832
    ♦ 4
    ♣ KJ9732

14) ♠ Q
    ♥ K943
    ♦ Q6532
    ♣ J42

15) ♠ KJ62
    ♥ Q432
    ♦ A4
    ♣ J62

ANSWERS TO QUIZ #III:

1) One Notrump. This is a "balanced" hand without a four-card major suit and 6 to 9 HCP.

2) One Heart. Even though the quality of our spade suit is better, we must bid our four-card major suits "up the line."

3) One Spade. Our first priority is to discover the 8-card major suit fit.

4) Two Clubs. We have the necessary 5-card support for our partner's club suit and 6 to 9 points.

5) One Diamond. Our hand is unbalanced and contains no 4-card major suit.

6) Three Clubs. A "limit raise" in Clubs showing 9 to 11 points.

7) Two Diamonds. Opener must have at least four diamonds to construct this auction. It is safer to play in our known eight-card fit than in a speculative notrump contract.

8) Two Hearts. This hand is very similar to #7, but here we have the safety of knowing we have at least a 7-card heart fit. We don't have to risk a notrump contract. We would like to use the *NEW MINOR FORCING* convention, but we don't possess the required <u>invitational strength</u> to activate the convention.

9) Two Notrump. An invitation with a flat hand.

10) Two Clubs. This is the *NEW MINOR FORCING* convention which helps to find 8-card major suit fits.

11) Two Clubs. Again, this is the *NEW MINOR FORCING* convention. Here we have a hand strong enough to force to game.

12) Two Hearts. We have found our 8-card major suit fit and have non-forcing values.

13) Three Clubs. Non-forcing and implying four hearts and six clubs. This is the *FUNNY JUMP*.

14) Two Diamonds. Non-forcing. We have the required 5-card diamond holding to retreat to our known 8-card fit.

15) Two Clubs. If our partnership bypass bidding a four-card spade suit to rebid One Notrump, we need to employ the *NEW MINOR FORCING* convention to find the eight-card spade fit.

or

Two Notrump. If our partnership would not bypass bidding a Notrumpfour-card spade suit in this sequence. There is no reason to explore for the eight-card spade fit that cannot exist.

CHAPTER 4

RESPONDING TO OPENING BIDS OF ONE OF A MAJOR WITHOUT A FIT

I. PRIORITIES

When your partner opens the bidding with a bid of One Heart or One Spade, your priorities are the same as if he had opened the bidding with a minor suit bid:

> 1) Look for the "golden fit" — eight cards in a major suit
> 2) Attempt to reach a notrump contract
> 3) Suggest playing the hand in a minor suit

If you have at least three-card support for your partner's major suit fit, it is relatively easy to communicate the fact that you have a fit and to tell your partner what the strength of your hand is. Those responses are discussed in the next chapter.

If you do not have a fit for your partner's major, but have the other major, it becomes necessary to embark upon a journey to discover whether or not your partner fits your major to the extent necessary to establish the "golden fit." How you do that depends upon 1) which major your partner opened and 2) the strength of your hand.

If your partner opens the bidding with One Heart and you do not have at least four hearts, but have at least four spades, it is likely you should respond One Spade no matter what the strength of your hand is. There are, of course, exceptions. The most notable exception and the one that is most affected by the fact that we are playing a two-over-one system occurs when you have exactly four spades and a lower-ranking suit of five-card length or longer **AND** have a hand of at least opening bid strength (12 HCP). We will soon see how to bid such a hand. But, for now, let us concern ourselves only with the hands of less than opening strength.

II. RESPONSES WITH LESS THAN 12 HCP

As we discussed above, when our partner opens with a bid of One Heart and we have four spades, we should bid One Spade. Not only does this enable us to find a fit if our partner also has four spades but it also helps us to find the right contract if our partner needs spade length to play notrump. In other words, it is the most descriptive bid available. If we have a "one-bid" hand (6 to 9 HCP), we probably will abide by our partner's decision concerning strain and level (his bid) over One Spade. We will either take a preference to the lowest possible heart contract if we have three hearts (with four hearts and four spades, we would have supported hearts immediately if systemically possible), pass his notrump bid (at the one, two or three level) or pass his bid of a second suit if we have at least four cards in the second bid suit and two or fewer hearts. With no fit for partner's second suit, we may take a preference to hearts with a doubleton.

With such minimum hands, passing a notrump rebid, taking a preference to our partner's first bid suit or passing his second-bid suit are not the only alternatives available to us. There is always the rebid of our own suit (non-forcing) and showing a six-card suit with virtually no support for our partner's suits. Or there is the "Funny Jump" (See FUNNY JUMPS). This conventional bid is a way of showing a weak hand with a four-card major and a six-card minor. And, of course, over an auction in which partner has bid two suits at the one level, such as:

NORTH	EAST	SOUTH	WEST
1♦	Pass	1♥	Pass
1♠	Pass	?	

there is always the One Notrump rebid by responder, showing 6 to 9 HCP with a "flat" hand or one which will deter the opponents from taking several tricks in the unbid suit. A typical hand with which the responder would rebid One Notrump in the above auction is shown in Example #36.

Example #36
♠ K2
♥ Q1063
♦ 94
♣ QJ954

III. THE FORCING NOTRUMP

Since we're not permitted to bid a lower-ranking suit in response to the opening bid of one of a major without game-going strength, the forcing notrump convention is employed. When we have a hand of less than opening strength (6 to 11 HCP) and cannot bid a suit at the one level (One Spade over One Heart), we must bid One Notrump. This bid is forcing for one round by an unpassed hand. Many partnerships play this bid as forcing or semi-forcing by a passed hand, also.

What statement does the bid of One Notrump make over the opening bid of one of a major? It says:

1) I do not have four spades (if the opening bid is One Heart);

2) I do not have 12 or more high card points and a biddable (five-card) lower-ranking suit;

3) I do not have a fit for your major unless I have a limit raise (9 to 11 points, with a "flat" hand).

More advanced partnerships utilize the forcing notrump with

more types of hands than those listed above. Our discussion while learning the convention will assume this limited definition and use.

IV. OPENER'S REBID AFTER A FORCING NOTRUMP

Without getting sidetracked on what opener **should** rebid over the forcing notrump, we will merely list opener's rebid and examine what **responder** should bid next.

OPENER MAY REBID HIS SUIT AT THE TWO LEVEL

This shows a six-card suit and a minimum opener (11 to 14 HCP). Responder usually passes. With a doubleton in opener's known six-card suit and invitational values, responder may raise to the three level (See CHAPTER 5). Responder should never "rescue" opener to a new suit. With Example #37, responder would pass a rebid of Two Spades by opener. With Example #38, responder may chose to raise to Three Spades, or, more conservatively, pass. With a third spade, responder shows his limit raise for opener's six-card major with a jump to game.

Example #37
♠ 2
♥ KJ9862
♦ Q4
♣ 9432

Example #38
♠ J6
♥ A642
♦ KJ4
♣ J832

OPENER MAY REBID TWO HEARTS AFTER OPENING THE BIDDING WITH ONE SPADE

Responder should initially assume opener has five spades and four hearts and should continue accordingly. He should take a

45

preference to spades with a doubleton spade and three or fewer hearts and less than 10 HCP. See Example #39. He should pass with four hearts, or with a singleton spade and at least a doubleton heart and less than 10 HCP. See Examples #40 and #41.

With 10 to 12 HCP and no fit for either major, he should rebid Two Notrump. See Example #42. Opener can then further describe his hand so the best final contract can be reached. Two NoTrump in this auction is one of the most descriptive bids that is available in the two-over-one system. It shows precisely less than three spades, less than four hearts and exactly 10 to 12 HCP, with reasonable cards in both minor suits.

OPENER MAY BID TWO CLUBS
OR TWO DIAMONDS

Example #39
♠ Q6
♥ J42
♦ K643
♣ Q1082

Example #40
♠ Q6
♥ J432
♦ K64
♣ Q1082

Example #41
♠ 6
♥ Q2
♦ J9842
♣ AJ742

Example #42
♠ Q2
♥ J43
♦ KQ72
♣ K962

When responder bids One Notrump over opener's opening bid of one of a major, he is not likely to have support for the major. Therefore, opener's duty is to seek a fit in another suit. If that suit is not the other major, it must be a minor suit. Therefore, the opener who does not have a six-card major to rebid (does not have a four-card heart suit if he has opened with One Spade) and who does not have a hand strong enough to raise to two or three Notrump will bid a minor suit. That suit will often be three cards in length. With 5-3-3-2 hand pattern and eleven to sixteen high-card points, opener will often need to show a three card minor as his rebid after a forcing notrump response. Therefore, the auction of:

NORTH	EAST	SOUTH	WEST
1♠	Pass	1NT	Pass
2♣			

often shows a three-card club suit. Example #43 is a typical opener's hand. Note that opener has three clubs and three diamonds. Opener should always bid clubs when he is 3-3 in the minors.

Example #43
♠ Q10872
♥ A4
♦ Q92
♣ AJ4

Responder has several options after opener's minor-suit rebid. If he makes a simple raise of opener's minor suit, he shows five-card support (remember that opener may have only three cards in the suit) and invitational strength (9 to 11 points).

There is a special opportunity to show a hand that has "grown up" to nearly forcing values after partner has opened with One Heart and rebid a minor suit over a forcing notrump. Responder can bid Two Spades to signal a five-card fit for the minor, and nearly game-forcing values. (Responder has denied holding spades with his forcing notrump call.) The auction would proceed

NORTH	EAST	SOUTH	WEST
1♥	Pass	1NT	Pass
2♣	Pass	2♠	

Example #44 shows such a hand.

Since two spades shows a good hand with a club fit, the partnership has a choice of meanings for a Three Club bid by responder. It can play the response as a "blocking bid," designed to keep the opponents out of the auction. Or it can play the Three Club bid as showing invitational values, slightly less strong than the Two Spade bid.

Example #44
♠ A6
♥ Q2
♦ J984
♣ KJ1092

If responder has the five-card support with a weak hand (6 to 9 points), he should pass unless the startling two spade bid is available.

If responder has the weak hand without five-card support, but a doubleton in opener's major suit, the auction would proceed:

NORTH	EAST	SOUTH	WEST
1♠	Pass	1NT	Pass
2♦	Pass	2♠	

with Example #45. Opener must be alert to the probability that responder is likely to have only a doubleton for his preference. Those who play constructive raises (See *CONSTRUCTIVE RAISES*) are more likely to have three or four trumps to produce this auction.

Example #45
- ♠ 83
- ♥ A64
- ♦ Q986
- ♣ J432

Example #46
- ♠ 4
- ♥ Q8
- ♦ K108432
- ♣ Q632

If responder has a weak hand without five-card support for opener's bid minor or without doubleton major suit support, he may bid a long suit of his own. With Example #46, the bidding might proceed:

Example #47
- ♠ 4
- ♥ K8
- ♦ KQ8432
- ♣ QJ43

NORTH	EAST	SOUTH	WEST
1♥	Pass	1NT	Pass
2♣	Pass	2♦	

With the same shape, but having invitational values (9 to 11 HCP), responder would jump to Three Diamonds. See Example #47.

With a relatively flat hand, that is, no six-card suit, invitational values (9 to 11 HCP) and no particular fit for either of opener's suits, responder would rebid two Notrump. Review Example #42.

48

These are bids that are made with flat hands — flat within the context of having a five-card major - and show specific quantities of high card points. A bid of Two Notrump shows 17 or 18 HCP. See Example #48. Different partnerships, in developing their <u>style</u> have defined these auctions differently, but, generally, these ranges are a good place to start. Responder must add these assumed values to his own and take the appropriate action - usually he will either pass Two Notrump or bid on to Three Notrump. A rebid by opener of Three Notrump shows a solid, long suit (propably six cards long) and some extra values - usually about 16 to 18 HCP. This bid is more of a "gambling," trick-taking description than a high-card point-showing bid. See Example #49. It also shows the hand one would have in the auction of:

Example #48
- ♠ K3
- ♥ AJ643
- ♦ KQJ
- ♣ A96

Example #49
- ♠ 2
- ♥ AKQJ62
- ♦ K64
- ♣ A43

Example #50
- ♠ K75
- ♥ Q42
- ♦ A62
- ♣ J853

NORTH	EAST	SOUTH	WEST
1♥	Pass	1♠	Pass
3NT			

Usually responder will pass the Three Notrump rebid by opener. There are two exceptions to this possible conclusion. The first occurs when responder has a flat limit raise in opener's major suit and was merely starting the auction with a "waiting bid" of One Notrump (See CHAPTER 5). In this case, responder should bid a game in opener's major suit. See Example #50. The correct bid over opener's rebid of Two or Three Notrump is Four Hearts.

The other exception occurs when responder has an unbalanced hand with one very long (six cards or longer) suit. In this case, responder may choose to "take out" the contract from notrump to his own suit. If he has a minimum hand without game-going values opposite his partner's known strength, he should make the minimum bid in his long suit. See Example #51. The auction should proceed:

Example #51
♠ 4
♥ Q63
♦ Q987432
♣ Q4

Example #52
♠ J6
♥ KJ9843
♦ Q62
♣ Q3

Example #53
♠ J6
♥ Q642
♦ Q
♣ KJ9843

NORTH	EAST	SOUTH	WEST
1♠	Pass	1NT	Pass
2NT	Pass	3♦	

Opener should pass responder's last bid.

If responder has an unbalanced hand with game-going values, he should bid a game in his suit. He knows opener has some support for him since opener has announced a relatively flat hand. He knows that the partnership has sufficient values to contract for a game. The only way he can convey this information is by bidding that game. See Example #52.

NORTH	EAST	SOUTH	WEST
1♠	Pass	1NT	Pass
2NT	Pass	4♥	

For Example #53:

NORTH	EAST	SOUTH	WEST
1♠	Pass	1NT	Pass
2NT	Pass	5♣	

50

If South had a six-card club suit, nine HCP and <u>no</u> singletons, he may choose to bid Three Notrump rather than Five Clubs.

OPENER MAY JUMP SHIFT

If opener has enough strength to force to game opposite a minimum One Notrump bid by responder <u>and</u> has an unbalanced hand he may jump shift into his second suit.

NORTH	EAST	SOUTH	WEST
1♠	Pass	1NT	Pass
3♦			

Example #54 and #55 shows a typical hand for opener. The jump shift bid is unconditionally forcing upon the responder.

Example #54
- ♠ KQJ93
- ♥ Q2
- ♦ AQJ82
- ♣ A

With a balanced hand he would instead bid Three Notrump.

Example #55
- ♠ KQJ932
- ♥ Q2
- ♦ AQJ8
- ♣ A

In the case where opener has one long suit and proper shape and values to commit to a game-level contract opposite any response from partner, he may be forced to make a jump shift into a "phony" suit. Example #56 shows such a hand.

Example #56
- ♠ AKJ10962
- ♥ Q
- ♦ KQ4
- ♣ KJ

The hand is not suited to a notrump contract. A bid of Three Spades is non-forcing and Four Spades would shut out investigation of a slam. Responder, of course, assumes opener is two-suited and bids accordingly. But, when opener's next bid is Four Spades, responder should suspect that opener's Three Diamond bid may have been merely an attempt to guarantee that the partnership reach a game-level contract in spades while showing a hand with some slam potential.

51

V. RESPONSES WITH HANDS OF INVITATIONAL STRENGTH (10 - 12 HCP)

The priorities continue to dictate our choice of bids for hands without a fit for our partner's major suit. If we have at least four spades, in response to our partner's opening bid of One Heart, we should bid One Spade with our 10 to 12 HCP. Without a four-card spade suit, we should respond with a bid of One Notrump — not necessarily because we are suggesting a no- trump contract — but because we are announcing a hand which contains fewer than four spades and strength of less than game-going values. The exception is the hand of 13 to 15 HCP that has no five-card suit. With such a hand, we would start with the bid of One Notrump and follow with a rebid of Three Notrump. If we are lucky enough to hold six or seven cards in a lower-ranking suit, we may use the forcing notrump, then bid that suit at the three level, or we may employ the *INVITATIONAL JUMP* explained in the *TOOLS & GADGETS* section.

So when we don't have a fit for our partner's major suit, but have a hand with "invitational" strength, we make the identical initial response that we would if our hand had minimum strength of 6 to 9 HCP. If we have a four-card spade suit, we respond with a bid of One Spade to our partner's One Heart opening; if we do not have at least four spades or, if our partner opens the bidding with One Spade, we start our series of responses with a bid of One Notrump (unless we have the *INVITATIONAL JUMP* hand discussed above and in the *TOOLS & GADGETS* section). The time to show the difference between the hands of minimum strength (6 to 9 HCP) and the hands of invitational strength (10 to 12 HCP) is during the <u>second round of bidding</u>.

Example #57
- ♠ 6
- ♥ KJ4
- ♦ Q10986
- ♣ AJ83

If our partner rebids his major suit, showing a six-card suit, and we have merely a singleton in his suit, and a relatively flat hand otherwise, we rebid Two Notrump. Example #57 is such a hand.

If our partner rebids a new, lower-ranking, suit at the two level such as:

NORTH	EAST	SOUTH	WEST
1♠	Pass	1NT	Pass
2♣	Pass	?	

or

NORTH	EAST	SOUTH	WEST
1♥	Pass	1♠	Pass
2♦	Pass	?	

once again, a bid of Two Notrump shows 10-12 HCP with no good fit for either of partner's suits. That is, a bid of Two Notrump announces that we have neither three cards in partner's major suit nor five-card support for his minor suit. In Standard methods, partner must have at least four cards in the minor suit to bid it. But, employing the Forcing Notrump, partner guarantees only three and, in a rare instance only two cards in the minor suit. Therefore, the responder must have five-card support to raise the bidding in that minor suit.

Similarly, in a "one-over-one-over-one" auction such as:

NORTH	EAST	SOUTH	WEST
1♦	Pass	1♥	Pass
1♠	Pass	?	

a bid of Two Notrump shows the invitational hand with no particularly good fit for either of partner's suits. Example #58 (a bad 12 HCP) is such a hand.

Example #58
♠ K42
♥ K963
♦ Q3
♣ KJ42

In this case, Two Notrump is a "jump bid" but has identical shape and values to the hands with which we rebid Two Notrump in

53

response to our partner's major-suit rebid or bid of a new, lower-ranking suit at the two level. These bids were not "jump bids."

VI. RESPONSES WITH 12 OR MORE HCP

All 12 HCP hands are not equal. Some are deemed to have opening bid values - others do not. This section deals with good 12 HCP hands as opposed to lesser 12 HCP hands discussed in the previous section. When our partner opens the bidding with one of a major suit and we have no fit and we have enough values to force to a game contract (12 or more HCP) our priorities continue to be:

1) Search for the "golden" major suit fit of eight cards;

2) Investigate the possibility of playing the hand in a notrump contract (In this case, at least Three Notrump)

3) Explore the possibility of playing the hand in a minor suit contract.

If we have no fit for our partner's major, how do we explore playing the hand in the other major? Obviously, if our partner opens the bidding with One Heart and we have at least four spades, we respond with a bid of One Spade. But what if our partner opened with a bid of One Spade and we want to suggest hearts as a strain for play? If we possess at least five hearts, we may respond with a bid of Two Hearts. This bid is forcing to game and shows at least a five-card heart suit. If our partner fits the heart suit (has at least three), he may raise hearts.

Being able to tell the difference between a "bad" hand and a "good" one is what separates a "bad" bridge player from a "good" one. The lack of minor suit controls would be a characteristic of a hand that would show little interest in a slam.

Example #59 would be such a hand. Opener would raise to Four Hearts which denies interest in a slam. With Example #60, however, we would bid only Three Hearts on the auction of:

NORTH	EAST	SOUTH	WEST
1♠	Pass	2♥	Pass
?			

because it hosts some features in the minor suits that would be valuable if a slam were attempted. Note that the two example hands have the identical number of high card points.

Example #59
- ♠ AQ632
- ♥ KQ4
- ♦ 872
- ♣ Q2

Responder, of course, may have a hand that is so good that he could not be discouraged from investigating loftier contracts. Particularly in marginal situations, opener's accurate account of the value of his own hand may steer the partnership to the correct level.

Example #60
- ♠ Q6432
- ♥ KQ6
- ♦ 8
- ♣ KQJ6

What if responder holds only four hearts? If we have a five-card minor suit, we start with a bid of that suit. In Example #61, we would respond to an opening bid of One Spade with a bid of Two Clubs. The Two Club bid says:

Example #61
- ♠ Q2
- ♥ AJ63
- ♦ 42
- ♣ KQJ92

1) I have game-going values.
2) Clubs is my longest suit.
3) I may or may not have another suit of four- card length.
4) I may or may not have a spade fit (See CHAPTER 5).

Armed with this information, opener must make the correct bid with his hand. With a fit (three or more cards) in clubs, he will raise clubs. Without a fit, but with four or more cards in a different suit, he will bid that suit. Perhaps that suit will be **hearts**. If he rebids Two Hearts, you may raise to Three Hearts. Thus, the heart fit is found even though his first bid and your first bid were not in hearts.

Remember: the Three Heart bid by responder is forcing because the Two Club bid committed the partnership to continue to bid until a game contract is reached.

There are hands where opener will have a four-card heart suit and will not rebid Two Hearts. The three types of hands which may be typical are:

1) A hand with six good spades, four bad hearts and minimum values. He will rebid Two Spades.

Example #62
♠ KJ962
♥ K1042
♦ AQ4
♣ Q

2) A hand with excellent notrump cards in the unbid suits. In the case of Example #62, hearts and diamonds. He will rebid Two Notrump.

3) A hand with a fit for the first suit responder bid. In the case of Example #63 he **may** bid Three Clubs. Although some would suggest that a bid of Two Hearts is correct.

Example #63
♠ KJ962
♥ K1042
♦ Q
♣ AQ4

Because opener may have one of these three types of hands, and thus, conceal his four-card heart suit, responder must rebid hearts at his next opportunity.

If we have four hearts, game-going values and do not have a five-card minor suit to bid, how do we start the exploration for the 4-4 heart fit? By bidding One Notrump. Typically, the Forcing Notrump bid is reserved for hands of five to eleven HCP. But, since our two-over-one bids are reserved for five-card or longer suits, we must extend the use of the Forcing Notrump to this strong hand which does not have a five-card suit. Not only would you start with a bid of One Notrump over partner's One Spade opener every time you had a four-card heart suit, at least twelve HCP and no five-card suit, but you would also bid One Notrump if you did not have four hearts, but met all the other requirements. Examples #64 and #65 would both be started with a One Notrump response over partner's One Spade. Over partner's rebid of Two Hearts, with Example #64 we would bid Four Hearts. With Example #65 we would bid Three Notrump.

After you have read CHAPTER 5, note that we should use either Two Notrump or Three Notrump over partner's One Spade opener as a **conventional** forcing raise. Therefore we cannot use that bid to indicate a game-going hand **without** a fit. Those partnerships which prefer the Two Notrump forcing raise should bid as suggested above when they possess twelve to fourteen HCP, no fit and no five-card suit. They first bid a Forcing Notrump, then jump to three notrump at the next turn.

Example #64

♠ J4
♥ AJ62
♦ KQ4
♣ K982

Example #65

♠ J4
♥ AJ6
♦ KQ42
♣ K982

An immediate response of three notrump in those partnerships should show the same shape, but fifteen to seventeen HCP.

In the partnerships which use Three Notrump as a forcing major-suit raise, Two Notrump may be used as a game-forcing hand without a five-card suit. But, if the partnership has a different use for the Two Notrump bid (a maximum limit raise, for example), it must bid as indicated above.

These are the ways that an eight-card heart fit can be discovered when the bidding is opened with One Spade and responder has game-going values.

VII. OPENER'S REBIDS AFTER A TWO-OVER-ONE RESPONSE

When opener and responder cannot combine for an eight-card major suit fit, a notrump contract is explored by natural bidding. When responder makes a two-over-one, announcing a five-card or longer suit and game-going values, opener rebids naturally. That is, he bids a new four-card suit if he has one, rebids his major if it is six cards long, raises responder's suit with three cards to an honor or rebids the correct number of notrump.

Examples #66 through #69 show various types of hands opener may have when responder bids Two Clubs after opener's One Spade bid. With Example #66 opener's rebid is Two Diamonds. With Example #67 opener's rebid is Two Spades. With Example #68 opener's rebid is Three Clubs. Examples #69 and #70 show hands where opener would rebid Two or Three Notrump.

In deciding whether or not to jump in notrump after responder's two-over-one, opener must determine whether he has a "minimum" hand or "extra values." With the minimum hand of Example #69, opener would rebid a mere two notrump. With extra values of Example #70, opener would jump to three notrump to show a hand of the 15

Example #66
- ♠ KJ842
- ♥ Q6
- ♦ AJ64
- ♣ Q2

Example #67
- ♠ KJ9842
- ♥ Q6
- ♦ AJ4
- ♣ Q2

Example #68
- ♠ KJ842
- ♥ Q63
- ♦ AJ
- ♣ Q62

Example #69
- ♠ KJ984
- ♥ K104
- ♦ AJ4
- ♣ Q6

Example #70
- ♠ KJ984
- ♥ K104
- ♦ AQ4
- ♣ K6

to 17 HCP range. With 18 or 19 HCP, opener would first rebid Two Notrump, then continue by bidding Four Notrump at his next turn.

Note that notrump rebids do not reflect the Principle of Fast Arrival.

If he raises Two Hearts to Three Hearts, opener shows at least three-card heart support and a hand that's good enough to suggest a slam. If he bids Four Hearts over our Two Hearts, he has at least three-card support and a hand that initially shows no interest in bidding toward a slam. Specifically, and by agreement, the hand holds no minor-suit controls. The manifestation of this difference between the Three Heart and the Four Heart bid is called the Principle of Fast Arrival. Simply stated, this axiom decrees that a jump to a game contract when it is not necessary, i.e., when a game-level contract has been "forced," (in this case, via a two-over-one bid by responder) denies interest in cue-bidding or exploring a contract higher than the game bid. The jump, therefore, shows a "bad" hand rather than a "good" one.

The fact that the partnership is committed to game influences opener's choice of rebids in **some** but not all situations. The primary difference between opener's rebids playing the two-over-one system and playing Standard methods is that, after responder's two-over-one bid, there is no longer the necessity to jump the bidding with a strong hand.

For example, playing Standard methods, with Example #71, the auction may proceed:

Example #71
- ♠ KQJ863
- ♥ A42
- ♦ Q83
- ♣ A4

NORTH	EAST	SOUTH	WEST
1♠	Pass	2♣	Pass
3♠			

Playing two-over-one, opener has a choice of rebids, depending on how his partnership elects to play. There is a diversity of opinion regarding the jump rebid by opener after responder's game-forcing two-over-one. One method is to play that a rebid of Three Spades in this auction shows a six-card spade suit and extra values — about 15 or more HCP. The theory is that this is the appropriate time in the auction for opener to announce his strength, facilitating succeeding bidding. Playing this method, Example #72 would be rebid Two Spades. Example #71 and #73 have sufficient values to be rebid Three Spades.

The other popular method is to play a Three Spade bid here to show a solid six-card suit, with or without extra values. The theory is that the advantage of playing a two-over-one system is to eliminate the necessity to jump, saving valuable bidding room. Therefore, an unnecessary jump should have a special meaning. And that meaning is to show six or more winners and no losers in the suit rebid.

Example #72
- ♠ AKQJ62
- ♥ 43
- ♦ Q42
- ♣ 32

Example #73
- ♠ AKQJ62
- ♥ A3
- ♦ Q75
- ♣ A2

If the partnership plays the jump rebid to show a solid suit, a simple rebid of Two Spades by opener does not show or deny any extra values. It merely shows a six-card spade suit. Playing this method, Example #71 would rebid Two Spades. Examples #72 and #73 would rebid Three Spades. (Note: There are exceptional hands where the Two Spade rebid is appropriate although opener has only five spades. But generally, the immediate rebid shows a six-card suit.)

Some Standard players promise at least one more bid as responder after a two-over-one (except over opener's limiting Two Notrump rebid). Others do not — especially after a "minimum" rebid of opener's suit. One of the joys players of the two-over one system find is that even in unfamiliar and unpracticed partnerships, they know that all bids are forcing after a two-over-one response. Therefore, whatever bid they make will not be passed.

It's not necessary for them to immediately evaluate their hands and make the "correct" value-showing bid.

In competitive auctions, the differences between Standard bidding and two-over-one bidding are even more pronounced. In Standard partnerships, the simple rebid is even more likely to be passed since opener has enough information (opponent's overcall and partner's two-over-one) to determine the value of his hand. The minimum rebid here is looked upon as a true value-showing bid rather than a "waiting" bid. The auction of:

NORTH	EAST	SOUTH	WEST
1♠	2♣	2♦	Pass
2♠			

does show a minimum hand in Standard methods whereas:

NORTH	EAST	SOUTH	WEST
1♠	Pass	2♣	Pass
2♠			

may or may not show a minimum, depending on whether the partnership plays that the two-over-one promises one more bid.

In keeping with our priorities when the major suit fit is ruled out, the search for a notrump contract is started. In general, after a two-over-one response, natural bidding is in effect for about one more round of bidding. For example:

NORTH	EAST	SOUTH	WEST
1♥	Pass	2♣	Pass
2♦	Pass	2♥	

would tell us a lot about both hands. We could be certain that North holds five hearts and four diamonds; he probably does not have three clubs to an honor (he may have immediately raised

61

clubs) and he probably does not have spades well-stopped for a notrump contract (he may have bid Two Notrump over two clubs, even with a four-card diamond suit). Responder probably has five or six clubs and precisely three hearts. If he had a four-card heart suit, he may have immediately chosen to make a conventional raise in hearts via a splinter or other conventional bid (See CHAPTER 5).

After the first two rounds of bidding, new suits are "suspect" because they are part of the investigation to reach a notrump contract. For example:

NORTH	EAST	SOUTH	EAST
1♠	Pass	2♦	Pass
2♠	Pass	3♦	Pass
3♥			

Here, Three Hearts may show a bad four-card heart suit, but is more likely to show good cards in the heart suit and a lack of good cards in the club suit. A typical hand for the auction would be Example #74. Since Three Notrump is so much more desirable a final contract than Five Diamonds, opener would bid Three Hearts rather than Four Diamonds. If responder has a club stopper, he should bid Three Notrump over Three Hearts. If he does not, he will bid something other than Three Notrump. Opener, with Example #74 should then drive toward a diamond game or slam, finding the least desirable of our priorities, the minor suit contract, the only feasible one.

Example #74

♠ AQJ862
♥ KQ4
♦ Q2
♣ J3

VIII. OPENER'S REVERSES AFTER A TWO-OVER-ONE

In Standard methods, a "reverse" bid by opener shows a good hand of 17 or more HCPs, a longer first suit, and is forcing at least one round. Playing two-over-one, opener's reverse after responder's one-over-one shows exactly those specific values and is forcing one round. The auction of:

NORTH	EAST	SOUTH	WEST
1♦	Pass	1♠	Pass
2♥			

Example #75

♠ K8
♥ AQ42
♦ KQJ63
♣ QJ

Example #76

♠ KJ1082
♥ Q7
♦ KQ83
♣ J9

shows at least a five-card diamond suit, at least a four-card heart suit and at least 17 HCP. A typical hand is shown in Example #75.

When responder makes a two-over-one bid, showing game-forcing values, it may not be necessary for opener to have such a strong hand in order to "bid out his pattern." There is a difference of opinion among bidding theorists concerning the strength opener must have in order to make a reverse bid after responder's game-forcing two-over-one. Some believe opener may reverse with minimum values. Others contend opener must have the standard 17 HCP. It seems the sanest approach may be to say that opener does not need the values required by a non-game-forcing two-over-one partnership, but he should not have a hand that is a dead minimum. That is, his reverse bids should show about 13 or more HCP.

When opener has a hand that is not well-suited to a notrump bid or a raise of responder's suit, or does not possess the required strength for a reverse, he may be forced into rebidding a five-card suit. The auction of:

NORTH	EAST	SOUTH	WEST
1♠	Pass	2♥	Pass
2♠			

is recommended for opener's hand in Example #76. Responder should suspect that opener may have only a five-card suit in such an auction.

QUIZ #IV

Partner opens the bidding with One Heart. What is our bid with each of the following hands?

1) ♠ J102   2) ♠ 932   3) ♠ 62   4) ♠ KQ82
    ♥ Q42   ♥ Q6   ♥ K   ♥ J4
    ♦ 8642   ♦ J1083   ♦ J9832   ♦ AJ1083
    ♣ AJ4   ♣ KQ75   ♣ Q9743   ♣ K4

We open the bidding with One Spade. Partner responds One Notrump. What is our next bid with each of the following hands?

5) ♠ Q10863   6) ♠ KJ932   7) ♠ KQ10972 8)♠ A9876
    ♥ A42   ♥ KQ   ♥ A2   ♥ J432
    ♦ K4   ♦ AJ4   ♦ Q42   ♦ KQ
    ♣ KJ2   ♣ KJ3   ♣ AJ   ♣ A8

Partner opens the bidding with One Spade. We bid One Notrump and he bids Two Clubs. What is our next bid with each of the following hands?

9) ♠ Q2   10)♠ J4   11)♠ 8   12)♠ J3
    ♥ 9762   ♥ KJ832   ♥ K92   ♥ AJ4
    ♦ Q98   ♦ 42   ♦ K108763   ♦ KQ93
    ♣ KQ82   ♣ Q1083   ♣ J43   ♣ 8732

We open the bidding with One Spade. Partner responds Two Hearts. What bid do we next make with each of the following hands?

13)♠ KQJ982 14)♠ AQ642 15)♠ KJ842 16)♠ KJ1092
    ♥ K   ♥ Q32   ♥ KJ   ♥ 4
    ♦ AQ4   ♦ Q2   ♦ J42   ♦ K83
    ♣ KJ4   ♣ QJ8   ♣ A103   ♣ AJ43

ANSWERS TO QUIZ #IV

1. Two Hearts. We know partner has at least five hearts. There is no reason to delay showing support.

2. One Notrump. Forcing. Unfortunately, this is a hand which makes us wish we were playing the NON-forcing Notrump. But, we're stuck with the system. If partner bids a minor suit, we will prefer to Two Hearts since his minor suit bid could be a three-card suit.

3. One Notrump. Forcing. Here we will pass partner's minor suit.

4. Two Diamonds. Game forcing. Here we have enough values for game. So, we should bid our longest suit first, even though we have a four-card spade suit. We can later explore for the 4-4 spade fit.

5. Two Clubs. Our second-longest suit. Although we also have three hearts, we must have at least four hearts to bid the suit.

6. Two Notrump. This rebid shows a balanced hand with 17 or 18 HCP.

7. Three Spades. Invitational. Showing a good 6-card suit and good values.

8. Two Hearts. Unlike bidding a minor, Two Hearts here shows at least four hearts.

9. Two Spades. We select the known 5-2 major suit as the trump fit rather than a possible 4-3 minor suit fit.

10. Two Spades. Here, again, we choose the known 5-2 major suit fit. We should not bid Two Hearts unless our partner-

ship has the understanding that opener can not pass with a singleton heart. If opener does have less than two hearts, he will bid Two Spades. Responder would be pleased to pass.

11. Two Diamonds. We are willing to play in our 6-? fit rather than a 5-1 spade fit or a 3-3 club fit.

12. Two Notrump. Showing no good fit for either of partner's suits, the unbid suits well-stopped and invitational values of 11 or 12 HCP.

13. Two Spades. Although we have a huge hand, we do not have a solid spade suit; therefore, we cannot jump to Three Spades if we play that Three Spades shows a solid suit.

or

Three Spades. But, if we play Three Spades shows extra values with or without a solid suit, we must bid Three Spades.

14. Four Hearts. Shows a heart fit, no minor suit controls, and no interest in a slam opposite a typical responder's hand.

15. Two Notrump. Even though we don't have diamonds well-stopped, we do have a flat minimum hand. We should not raise hearts without at least three cards in the suit.

16. Two Spades. This is the one time we must rebid a poor five-card suit. Our hand is not immediately well-suited to notrump because of our singleton heart. We would like to bid our second suit - clubs - but we have such a minimum hand we can't stand to elevate the level of bidding beyond the two level. Although "reverses" do not show lots of extra values opposite responder's game-forcing two-over-one, bidding Three Clubs here would deny the minimum hand we have.

CHAPTER 5

RESPONDING TO OPENING BIDS OF ONE OF A MAJOR SUIT WITH A FIT

I. PRIORITIES

Once again, our priorities remain the same:

1) Identify the "golden fit" of eight cards in a major suit

2) Search for a notrump contract

3) Seek and establish a fit in a minor suit

When we know that, as a partnership, we have found an eight-card major suit fit, the easiest way to continue the auction to determine what level we should reach is by telling our partner, as soon as possible, that we have a fit.

II. SIMPLE MAJOR SUIT RAISES

With weak hands a simple raise conveys the necessary information — we have at least 3-card support for our partner's major and 6 to 9 **total** points. As our sophistication increases, we will find ways to differentiate between the "distributional" simple raise and the "flat" simple raise, and between the very weak simple raise (5 to 7 points) and the "constructive" simple raise (8 to 9 points). See *CONSTRUCTIVE RAISES*. For the time being, the auction:

NORTH	EAST	SOUTH
1♠	Pass	2♠

or

NORTH	EAST	SOUTH
1♠	2♦	2♠

shows the 6 to 9 point hand with a fit.

III. THE SEARCH FOR THE 4-4 MAJOR SUIT FIT

The only exception to the rule that you should immediately raise your partner's major to the two level when you have 6 to 9 points and at least a three-card fit is when you have four cards in the other major suit and three cards in your partner's suit. Since, when you have a choice of eight-card fits, it is better to play in the 4-4 fit rather than the 5-3 fit, you should respond to your partner's opening bid of One Heart with a bid of One Spade. If your partner has four spades, you will find the 4-4 fit. If your partner does not raise spades, you can show the three-card heart support on the next round of bidding. Those who play the Flannery convention may elect to respond with a bid of One Spade to their partner's opening One Heart bid only when they have at least five spades. They know if their partner had four spades and five hearts and a minimum opener, he would open with a conventional bid of Two Diamonds.

When our partner opens the bidding with One Spade and we have exactly three spades and exactly four hearts, we may want to explore the possibility that partner has a four-card heart suit as well as his announced five-card spade suit so that we may play in our 4-4 heart fit rather than in our 5-3 spade fit. When the strength of our hand prevents us from making a two-over-one bid, the only method available to us to search for partner's "other" or "secondary" suit is by bidding One Notrump (forcing). Hence, with Example #77, the auction would proceed:

NORTH	EAST	SOUTH
1♠	Pass	1NT

If partner does not rebid Two Hearts, we will show spade support with minimum values by bidding Two Spades. If our partner surprises us by bidding Two Hearts, we would be pleased to pass because we have successfully uncovered the 4-4 major suit fit. If partner shows extra strength by bidding something other than Two Clubs or Two Diamonds, we would bid the cheapest available number of spades if we were at the lower range of our simple raise, and would bid Four Spades if at the top of our range. For example:

Example #77
♠ J83
♥ QJ94
♦ 84
♣ K732

NORTH	EAST	SOUTH	WEST
1♠	Pass	1NT	Pass
2NT	Pass	?	

With Example #77 we would bid Three Spades; with Example #78 we would bid Four Spades. Also:

NORTH	EAST	SOUTH	WEST
1♠	Pass	1NT	Pass
3♦	Pass	?	

Example #78
♠ K83
♥ KJ42
♦ Q4
♣ Q743

Again, with Example #77 we would bid Three Spades; with Example #78 we would bid Four Spades.

The principles discussed above for finding a 4-4 major suit fit when we know we have a 5-3 fit in the other major also apply to hands of strength greater than 6 to 9 points. With hands of unlimited strength, we would generally respond One Spade to partner's One Heart opening bid every time we held four spades and three hearts. And, with invitational (10 to 12 points) or game-forcing (13 or more points) hands with three spades and four hearts, we would generally respond One Notrump to partner's One Spade opening bid in the hope of uncovering the desired 4-4 heart fit. See Examples #79 and #80. In each case we would bid One Notrump in response to partner's opening bid of One Spade.

As you can see, our sophistication has reached the point where it is no longer sufficient to satisfy the number one priority of finding the eight-card major suit fit; even if we are assured of having a 5-3 fit we embark upon an exploration for the superior 4-4 fit. When we determine that the 4-4 fit in the other major suit does not exist, we then "place" the contract in our partner's major suit.

Example #79
♠ K82
♥ QJ83
♦ Q64
♣ K82

Example #80
♠ KJ4
♥ K832
♦ AJ
♣ Q842

IV. RAISES WITH INVITATIONAL HANDS (10 TO 12 POINTS)

Most two-over-one partnerships (and every **good** partnership) have adopted a specific major suit raise structure. A series of bids (or bidding "system") has been constructed for every strength and shape of hand the responder may have which has a fit for opener's major suit. Some of these "systems" are less straight forward than others. There is a system which highly values the pre-emptive jump raise with a weak hand and a fit. For the time being, we will concentrate on describing the "standard" two-over-one system for describing hands with fits. We have already seen that weak hands, hands with 6 to 9 total points, are described by giving **simple** raises from One Spade to Two Spades.

Hands which have invitational values (10 to 12 points) are

candidates for a **limit** jump raise from One Spade to Three Spades. Hence:

NORTH	EAST	SOUTH
1♠	Pass	3♠

or

NORTH	EAST	SOUTH
1♠	2♣	3♠

shows a hand with at least three-card support for the spade suit and 10 to 12 points. Remember: when we have a fit we count **total** points which are the sum of high card points and distributional points. Example #81 is a hand with which we would bid Three Spades in both auctions above.

In an effort to be even more descriptive than establishing the difference among "weak," "invitational" and "forcing" hands and raises, bridge theorists have decided that there are basically two types of "invitational" hands: those hands that have invitational values due to the fact they have 10 to 12 HCP and those hands that are "invitational" because they possess 10 to 12 points, largely due to their **distributional** values. These same theorists believe it is important to distinguish between these two types of hands and have constructed a way to show each of them by using specific bidding sequences.

Example #81

♠ Q832
♥ A42
♦ KJ84
♣ J6

Example #82

♠ Q432
♥ 83
♦ KQJ64
♣ 43

The invitational hand which gains its value by virtue of distribution is called a "distributional limit raise" and is described by the immediate jump. The two auctions cited above would describe a hand with 10 to 12 points, several of which are due to the presence of short suits — distribution. Example #82 is such a hand.

The other type of invitational hand is know as the "flat" limit raise and cannot be described by the immediate jump.

Example #83 is such a hand. It is shown by, without interference, starting the response structure with the bid of One Notrump (forcing), and then jumping to Three Spades. This series of bids shows the flat limit raise. Hence:

Example #83
- ♠ Q432
- ♥ Q63
- ♦ KJ96
- ♣ Q4

Example #84
- ♠ K863
- ♥ Q63
- ♦ A42
- ♣ Q32

NORTH	EAST	SOUTH	WEST
1♠	Pass	1NT	Pass
2♣	Pass	3♠	

shows such a hand.

When partner foils our plan to jump on the second round of bidding by bidding something other than two of a lower-ranking suit, we must adapt. If he rebids Two Spades, our raise to Four Spades would show the flat limit raise. If he rebids Two Notrump, our jump to Four Spades would show the flat limit raise. If he jump rebids Three Spades, a new suit would be a cue bid and would show the flat limit raise.

NORTH	EAST	SOUTH	WEST
1♠	Pass	1NT	Pass
3♠	Pass	4♦	

shows a hand similar to Example #84.

V. PRE-EMPTIVE JUMP RAISES IN COMPETITION

One modern treatment used by many two-over-one players is the pre-emptive jump raise in competition. In an auction where partner opens the bidding with one of a major, and right hand opponent makes a simple overcall, a jump raise is no longer the limit raise of 9 to 11 points previously described in this chapter.

NORTH	EAST	SOUTH	WEST
1♠	2♦	3♠	

Using this treatment, the jump raise would show values in the 3 to 7 point raise, with some "extra" distribution which would exceed the "flat" distribution of a simple raise. Example #85 shows a hand with which we would make a **pre-emptive jump raise.** Example #86 shows a hand with which we would make a simple raise. If we adopt this method, how do we now make a limit raise, showing 9 to 11 points? By **cue-bidding.** Hence, the auction of

Example #85
- ♠ J842
- ♥ J732
- ♦ 8
- ♣ KJ32

Example #86
- ♠ J842
- ♥ Q64
- ♦ 84
- ♣ KJ32

NORTH	EAST	SOUTH	WEST
1♠	2♦	3♦	

would usually show a limit raise or better in spades. We are showing anywhere from 9 to an unlimited number of points **and** a spade fit for partner. Opener's rebid opposite this cue-bid must now reflect his strength opposite an assumed minimum limit raise. In other words, he would jump to game with a hand strong enough to accept the invitation of a limit raise. He would cue bid a new suit if he were interested in a slam opposite the same minimum limit raise. He would "sign off" at the three level with a minimum hand of his own.

VI. RAISES WITH GAME-GOING VALUES AND A FIT

Since there are several types of hands which have game-going values and a fit for partner's major suit, there are several methods of raising partner's major. These methods may be divided into two primary categories: immediate raises and delayed raises.

IMMEDIATE RAISES

When partner opens the bidding with One Heart or One Spade and we have support for his suit and at least 12 total points, we may tell him so by making a **conventional** bid which makes that precise statement. Popular conventional forcing raise bids are Three Notrump and Two Notrump. Using the Three Notrump conventional raise the auction of

NORTH	EAST	SOUTH	WEST
1♥	Pass	3NT	

says "Partner, I have support for you and a game-forcing hand." "Support" is defined by some partnerships as a four-card holding. Other partnerships define "support" as a three-card holding. Those "four-card holding" partnerships would use a much lengthier auction to show support for partner's major with only three-card support; in other words, they would make a delayed forcing raise. We will soon discuss delayed forcing raises. "Three-card holding" partnerships usually stipulate that the hand must have **some** distribution, some short suit(s), which make the hand a trump-suit playing hand rather than a notrump hand.

After the Three Notrump raise by responder, opener would show a minimum hand by "signing off" with a bid of game in the trump suit:

NORTH	EAST	SOUTH	WEST
1♥	Pass	3NT	Pass
4♥			

With more than a minimum hand, opener may elect to start a cue-bidding sequence:

NORTH	EAST	SOUTH	WEST
1♥	Pass	3NT	Pass
4♣			

Although most partnerships would play the bid of Four Clubs as showing the ace of clubs and more than a minimum hand, some would prefer that the Four Club bid showed a second suit and an interest in slam. Example #87 would be such a hand.

Example #87
♠ Q4
♥ KQJ93
♦ A
♣ KJ1082

In summary, after a Three Notrump bid by responder as a forcing raise, opener should rebid the trump suit at the four level with all minimum hands and should bid a new suit with a forward-going hand that has some potential for slam opposite a typical forcing raise hand.

THE TWO NOTRUMP FORCING RAISE

Primarily to provide more bidding room, the Forcing Two Notrump Raise (popularly known as the <u>Jacoby Two Notrump</u>) is employed by many more good partnerships than the Three Notrump raise. The sequence of

NORTH	EAST	SOUTH	WEST
1♠	Pass	2NT	

shows a hand with game-going values and support for partner's major suit. The same definition of "support" applies here as mentioned above. Most expert partnerships require four-card support for this conventional use.

With the forcing Two Notrump bid, opener's rebids are much more structured and inflexible. There is a specific meaning to each of opener's rebids. Summarized here, jumps to game in the trump suit show minimum hands with no singletons or voids. Three level bids show shortness in the bid suit. Other bids show more than a minimum opener. The Two Notrump bid starts the partnership down a well-defined path.

DELAYED FORCING MAJOR SUIT RAISES

When opener starts the auction with the bid of one of a major and the responder has game-going values with a fit for that major suit, he may immediately convey that information or he may delay conveying it, depending on the shape of his hand. One of the attractions of the two-over-one system is that natural bidding is expected, especially in the early stages of the auction. Therefore, responder would bid his longest suit at the cheapest level as his first response. So, the auction of

NORTH	EAST	SOUTH	WEST
1♥	Pass	2♣	

or

NORTH	EAST	SOUTH	WEST
1♥	2♣	2♦	

would show game-going values and a five-card or longer bid suit. A preliminary assumption is that responder does **not** have a fit for opener's major; otherwise, he would have raised the major immediately (or cue bid in the case of interference). But, responder **may** have a raise, particularly with three-card support, and a five-card suit in the suit he bids. Opener rebids as if responder does not have a fit. Example #88 and Example #89 are hands with which responder would bid Two Diamonds in response to opener's opening bid of One Heart. Notice that one of these hand contains a fit for partner's heart suit and the other does not. The fit for partner's major can be disclosed during the next round of bidding. After the auction of

Example #88
- ♠ AK
- ♥ 2
- ♦ KQJ842
- ♣ Q753

Example #89
- ♠ 84
- ♥ AQ10
- ♦ AKJ103
- ♣ Q42

Example #90
- ♠ A2
- ♥ KJ863
- ♦ Q4
- ♣ K1083

NORTH	EAST	SOUTH	WEST
1♥	Pass	2♦	Pass
3♣	Pass	3♥	

opener will know

1) Responder has game-going values.

2) Responder has at least five diamonds.

3) Responder has at least three hearts.

Notice that opener knew #1 and #2 after the Two Diamond bid. Armed with this extensive amount of information, opener can proceed intelligently. For instance, with Example #90 opener may well consider investigating a heart slam, since he can envision a long diamond suit to provide winners for his black suit losers. If responder had made a forcing raise in hearts immediately without telling opener he had a five-card diamond suit, opener may not have considered investigation of a slam. Some say this is a strength of the two-over-one system; it isn't so much that responder wouldn't bid Two Diamonds playing Standard methods, but the fact that he would have to jump to **Four** Hearts on the second round of bidding would make opener more reluctant to investigate slam by having to cue bid at the four or five level. Playing two-over-one, opener, can make the same investigation, but at the three or four level. Once again, with Example #90 opener could and **should** bid Three Spades over Three **game-forcing** Hearts in the example auction. He would be reluctant to bid Four Spades over Four Hearts playing Standard methods, particularly with his own minimum values. Yet, if Examples #89 and #90 are the responder's and opener's hands, six hearts is a virtual laydown without a finesse and with any opening lead (other than a 7-0 or 6-1 club distribution which would allow the defense a ruff).

QUIZ #V

Partner opens the bidding with One Spade. What do you respond with each of the following hands?

1) ♠ Q32
   ♥ 42
   ♦ K865
   ♣ Q987

2) ♠ Q32
   ♥ J843
   ♦ K8
   ♣ Q963

3) ♠ J983
   ♥ K4
   ♦ QJ87
   ♣ K92

4) ♠ J983
   ♥ 4
   ♦ KQ87
   ♣ KJ92

5) ♠ KQ82
   ♥ AJ9
   ♦ Q432
   ♣ Q4

6) ♠ KQ2
   ♥ AJ94
   ♦ Q432
   ♣ Q4

7) ♠ QJ9
   ♥ Q2
   ♦ AQ832
   ♣ K84

8) ♠ Q983
   ♥ 2
   ♦ K863
   ♣ 9863

ANSWERS TO QUIZ #V

1) Two Spades. This bid shows 6 to 9 points and at least 3-card support.

2) One Notrump. Forcing. We are seeking the 4-4 heart fit. If partner does not bid hearts, we will prefer to spades.

3) One Notrump. We are preparing to show the "flat" limit raise. If partner bids Two clubs, Diamonds or Hearts, we will bid Three Spades.

4) Three Spades. This shows an "unbalanced" limit raise.

5) Two Notrump (Jacoby Forcing Raise) or Three Notrump (Forcing Raise). This is a hand with which we want to make a _conventional_ forcing raise. We have 12 to 15 points and a fit. Some would make a two-over-one bid of Two Diamonds, and then raise spades. But it is not recommended that we make a two-over-one in a four-card suit; we should have at least a five-card suit.

6) One Notrump. As in Answer #2 above, we are seeking the 4-4 heart fit. The only difference here is that we have game-forcing values which we will announce on the next round of bidding.

7) Two Diamonds. We have sufficient values and a suit of adequate length to make a game-forcing two-over-one bid. The fact that we also have support for our partner's major suit will be disclosed in a later round of bidding.

8) Two Spades. By adding points for distribution, we can scrape up a response. If we were playing "pre-emptive jump raises in competition," and there was a simple overcall by our right hand opponent, this hand would qualify for a Three Spade bid.

PART II

TOOLS &
GADGETS

There are many, many conventions and treatments which can be used to enhance a bidding system. Most of these enhancements can be incorporated into any system, whether that system is two-over-one, Precision, Standard, or any other. Part II will familiarize us with the conventions and treatments which are virtually essential to playing a complete two-over-one system or which are particularly valuable because we are playing two-over-one. Part II will not list or describe all available treatments and conventions - just the most necessary ones.

TWO-OVER-ONE "OFF IN COMPETITION"

The discussions in Part I stated that, when a new lower-ranking suit was named at the two level in response to our partner's opening bid of one of a suit, the partnership was unequivocally committed to continue bidding until a game contract was reached.

Negative doubles (see *NEGATIVE DOUBLES*) may be used to "bid" lower-ranking suits without forcing to game. But, for some players, this is not enough. They feel that a negative double, although unlimited in strength, makes the statement that the responder has limited length in the unbid suits or, more specifically, has no more that five cards in any unbid major suit. A good example of this principle is shown by

```
♠ Q2
♥ KJ963
♦ A42
♣ 832
```

In the auction

NORTH	EAST	SOUTH	WEST
1♠	2♣	?	

players who play "pure" two-over-one or, in other words, "two-over-one **on** in competition," would make a negative double, stating

1. I have nine or more points.

2. I have four or more hearts.

But some players would prefer to bid Two-Hearts stating

1. I have nine or more points (but not necessarily enough to force to game).

2. I have five or more hearts.

Thus, the partnership can find a 5-3 heart fit they may miss if a negative double were employed. Since the opener can only rely on values of nine HCP by the responder, he must be careful to make the correct rebid after his partner's Two Heart bid. For example, playing two-over-one "on," opener's rebid of Two Notrump shows unlimited values (12 or more HCP). But, playing two-over-one "off," opener's rebid of Two Notrump is limited to between 12 and 15 HCP. Since responder may have as little as 9 HCP and would pass Two Notrump with 9 or 10 HCP, opener must jump to Three Notrump with sufficient game-going values opposite those 9 or 10 HCP. In other words, Three Notrump shows 16 to 18 HCP. In such a case opener's hand could be

♠ KJ962
♥ A2
♦ KQ4
♣ K62

Since responder's two-over-one may show an extremely strong hand as well as the minimum hand of 9 HCP, the bid of a new suit at the two level by the responder is forcing for one round, even playing two-over-one **off** in competition.

CONSTRUCTIVE RAISES

One of the benefits of having the Forcing Notrump available for use over partner's opening bid of one of a major, is that it provides one more step for description of responder's shape and size. In other words, without playing a forcing notrump, immediate simple raises have a relatively broad range:

NORTH	EAST	SOUTH	WEST
1♠	Pass	2♠	

shows six to nine points

NORTH	EAST	SOUTH	WEST
1♠	Double	2♠	

shows three to seven points

NORTH	EAST	SOUTH	WEST
1♠	2♣	2♠	

shows six to nine points

By incorporating the Forcing Notrump into the first of these simple raise sequences, we are better able to define the strength of our hand; we can differentiate between the six or seven point simple raise and the eight or nine point simple raise.

Playing the "Constructive Major Suit Raises" treatment, an immediate simple raise in "free" (without interference) auctions shows the higher range (eight or nine points) of our possible strength. So:

NORTH	EAST	SOUTH	WEST
1♠	Pass	2♠	

shows eight or nine points. Auctions which go through the Forcing Notrump and "preference" to Two Spades show the hand of six or seven points with a fit (3 or 4 spades) or a doubleton. So, with the lower range of possible strength hands, the auction would proceed:

NORTH	EAST	SOUTH	WEST
1♠	Pass	1NT	Pass
2♣, 2♦ or 2♥	Pass	2♠	

This auction shows either the lower range of the simple raise OR a doubleton spade with a weak (6 to 9 points) hand. Because with

♠ Q832
♥ J42
♦ K873
♣ 84

the auction would proceed as above. And, with

♠ 82
♥ KJ2
♦ Q432
♣ J963

an identical auction would ensue. How does opener know which type of hand responder has? The answer is: Opener does not know. Opener only needs to find out when he has an unusually strong hand, either in high card points or in distribution. In either case, opener will make an additional bid, asking responder which type of hand he has. And responder will answer appropriately.

With

♠ KJ965
♥ A
♦ A2
♣ K10752

opener can envision bidding a game in spades if responder has at least three spades and a fit in clubs. So the auction would proceed:

NORTH	EAST	SOUTH	WEST
1♠	Pass	1NT	Pass
2♣	Pass	2♠	Pass
3♣	Pass	?	

With the three or four-card spade fit, and a favorable holding in the club suit, responder would jump to Four Spades, With the long spades and an unfavorable holding in clubs, responder would bid **only** Three Spades. With a doubleton spade and longer clubs, responder could pass with minimum values.

With extra high card points, and a "flat" hand, opener would make a game try by bidding Two Notrump:

♠ AJ932
♥ KQ2
♦ QJ
♣ KQ

Responder would sign off in Three Spades if he held the minimum (6 or 7 points) hand with the spade fit. Or he would pass with a minimum hand without spades (a doubleton) or bid Three Notrump with a relatively "good" hand (8 or 9 points) without a fit. With the maximum hand and a spade fit he would have bid Two Spades immediately.

How does interference bidding affect our ability to show the very weak or the constructive raise? In the face of a simple overcall we cannot find a way of bidding each of the two types of simple raise hands differently. Therefore, in the auction of

NORTH	EAST	SOUTH	WEST
1♥	2♣	2♥	

the bid of Two Hearts has a relatively broad range of 6 to 9 points. Unless we are playing a Pre-emptive Jump Raise in Competition structure. In that case, the bid of Two Hearts tends to show the top end of the possible range.

But over takeout doubles there is a method to differentiate between the good simple raise and the poor simple raise. That method is to make the simple raise with the poor hand and to bid Two Clubs with the constructive raise. If responder is a passed hand, the Two Diamond bid is substituted for the Two Club bid to show the constructive raise so that Two Clubs can be used as a Drury bid (see *DRURY*). Therefore,

NORTH	EAST	SOUTH	WEST
1♠	Double	2♠	

and

NORTH	EAST	SOUTH	WEST
		Pass	Pass
1♠	Double	2♠	

show the weak raise and

NORTH	EAST	SOUTH	WEST
1♠	Double	2♣	

and

NORTH	EAST	SOUTH	WEST
		Pass	Pass
1♠	Double	2♦	

show the constructive raise.

The negatives attached to adopting "Constructive Major Raises" into your bidding agreements must also be considered. When responder has a minimum raise with a fit, he must respond by using the forcing notrump. This allows opponents to enter the auction at the two level. Had responder been able to raise opener's major suit with minimum values the opponent next to speak might be pre-empted and unable to bid at the three level. Also, when responder does use the forcing notrump and prefers to opener's major at the two level, opener does not know whether responder has a fit with sparse values (6 or 7 points), or a doubleton with the possiblity of greater values (as much as 9 points).

FOURTH SUIT FORCING

We understand that one primary advantage of the two-over-one system is that, once we make a two-over-one bid, we can subsequently make weak-sounding bids such as preferences or rebids of our own suits, but are still unequivocally committed to continue bidding until a game contract is reached. For example,

NORTH	EAST	SOUTH	WEST
1♥	Pass	2♣	Pass
2♦	Pass	2♥	

or

NORTH	EAST	SOUTH	WEST
1♥	Pass	2♣	Pass
2♦	Pass	3♣	

These sequences may sound weak, but they cannot be passed. But what happens when responder did not start with a two-over-one, but wants to force to game, and either show extra length in his own suit or show a delayed fit for partner's suit? Jumps are invitational. Such as

NORTH	EAST	SOUTH	WEST
1♥	Pass	1♠	Pass
2♣	Pass	3♥	

or

NORTH	EAST	SOUTH	WEST
1♥	Pass	1♠	Pass
2♣	Pass	3♥	

Non-jumps are sign-offs:

NORTH	EAST	SOUTH	WEST
1♥	Pass	1♠	Pass
2♣	Pass	2♥	

or

NORTH	EAST	SOUTH	WEST
1♥	Pass	1♠	Pass
2♣	Pass	2♠	

If opener rebids 1NT, we have the New Minor Forcing Convention to utilize. But what if opener does not rebid 1NT? Instead, opener rebids a new suit- non-forcing. It is at this crossroad in the bidding that we can employ the Fourth Suit Forcing convention. What bidding the fourth, or unbid, suit does is commit the partnership to a game contract so that ensuing minimum or space-saving bids will not end the auction.

NORTH	EAST	SOUTH	WEST
1♥	Pass	1♠	Pass
2♣	Pass	2♦	

says nothing about the diamond suit. It merely says "Partner, we must continue bidding until we reach a game level contract. I will later tell you more about my hand. I may have an extra-long spade suit; or I may have only four spades and a heart fit for you. Or I may have a club fit. But one thing is certain: We must continue to bid until a game contract is reached. Now, since you must continue bidding, why don't you make the most descriptive bid you can?" (Some pairs agree to use Fourth Suit Forcing in invitational auctions as well. This usage requires specific agreements to show the difference between invitational and game forcing hands as the auction continues).

Opener's next bid is a reflection of the priorities we have mentioned so often:

1) Find an eight-card major suit fit. With three-card support for responder's spade suit in the auction above opener would bid Two Spades.

2) Reach a notrump contract. If opener does not have three spades, but otherwise has a relatively flat hand with diamonds (the fourth suit) stopped, he should bid Two Notrump.

3) Find a minor suit contract. Without three spades and with no diamond stopper, opener would rebid a five-card club suit or, if he had only four clubs, would rebid a very good five-card heart suit.

With

♠ Q42
♥ AJ983
♦ 6
♣ KQJ4

the auction would proceed:

NORTH	EAST	SOUTH	WEST
1♥	Pass	1♠	Pass
2♣	Pass	2♦	Pass
2♠			

With

♠ 82
♥ AJ983
♦ K6
♣ KQJ4

the auction would be

NORTH	EAST	SOUTH	WEST
1♥	Pass	1♠	Pass
2♣	Pass	2♦	Pass
2NT			

With

♠ 82
♥ AJ983
♦ 6
♣ KQJ42

the bidding should go

NORTH	EAST	SOUTH	WEST
1♥	Pass	1♠	Pass
2♣	Pass	2♦	Pass
3♣			

With

♠ 8
♥ AQJ83
♦ 432
♣ KQJ2

the bidding would be

NORTH	EAST	SOUTH	WEST
1♥	Pass	1♠	Pass
2♣	Pass	2♦	Pass
2♥			

Here Two Hearts does not guarantee a six-card suit. It merely shows a hand that can not satisfy the requirements for any higher-priority action. That is, it can not support spades, it cannot bid notrump since it has no diamond stopper, and it can not rebid clubs. If opener has a good stopper in the "unbid" fourth suit, he can bid Two Notrump. If he holds

♠ AJ832
♥ K42
♦ AQ83
♣ 6

the auction would proceed

NORTH	EAST	SOUTH	WEST
1♠	Pass	2♣	Pass
2♦	Pass	2♥	Pass
2NT			

If he has

♠ AJ832
♥ J2
♦ AQ83
♣ Q4

the auction would proceed

NORTH	EAST	SOUTH	WEST
1♠	Pass	2♣	Pass
2♦	Pass	2♥	Pass
3♣ or 3♥			

A bid of Three Clubs shows less support than an immediate raise. Opener has three small clubs or a doubleton honor. A bid of Three Hearts shows a partial heart stopper for notrump.

When contemplating the utility of the Fourth Suit Forcing convention, it is easy to think of the New Minor Forcing Convention. Both conventions bid a suit artificially to check back for support for responder's suit. But the New Minor Forcing Convention is used only over opener's rebid of One Notrump and is not forcing to game. Fourth Suit forcing is used over opener's bid of a new suit and is usually played as forcing to game.

One-over-one auctions are not the only ones that can employ Fourth Suit Forcing. There are some two-over-one (game forcing) auctions that also use the fourth suit bid as an artificial one. Let's say you hold:

♠ Q4
♥ Q32
♦ J63
♣ AKJ104

and the auction proceeds

NORTH	EAST	SOUTH	WEST
1♠	Pass	2♣	Pass
2♦	Pass	?	

What is your next bid? Bidding Two Spades shows three card support. You can't raise Two Diamonds to three without better and longer diamonds. You have only five clubs so you should not rebid them. Your heart stopper is tenuous. The opponents are very likely to lead a heart against a notrump contract, embarassing your holding in that suit. The answer is to bid Two Hearts-Fourth Suit Forcing. It's not as much a check back for support for your suit (you could bid Three Clubs - if you had extra long clubs) as it is a statement that you have none of the higher-priority items to show. You don't have good support for either of opener's suits. Note that a delayed raise in responder's two-over-one suit requires only a good two cards, whereas delayed support for responder's one-over-one suit requires three cards. Also, in the auction above, if opener wants to supress announcing support for responder's suit, he can bid Three Hearts which tends to deny good heart cards for a notrump contract (he would bid Notrump with good hearts) and asks responder to bid Notrump with a partial heart stopper.

FUNNY JUMPS

A compelling tenet of the two-over-one system is the fact that the search for the eight-card major suit fit is of primary importance. Therefore, when opener starts the bidding with One Club or One Diamond, responder's first duty is to start down the path toward discovery of the eight-card major suit fit; he must bid a four card major suit if he has one UNLESS HE HAS THE NECESSARY STRENGTH TO FORCE TO GAME AND HE HAS A SUIT LONGER THAN HIS 4-CARD MAJOR. For example, with

> ♠ 8
> ♥ J842
> ♦ KQJ832
> ♣ 62

responder would bid One Heart as a response to his partner's One Club opening; with

> ♠ 8
> ♥ KQ42
> ♦ AJ9432
> ♣ K7

responder would bid One Diamond, because his extra strength allows him to explore for the 4-4 heart fit later.

Another way of looking at all this is that, if responder does not have game-forcing values, he must bid his 4-card major rather than bidding his five or six-card minor suit. When opener rebids One Notrump, responder can not bid his minor suit without the auction being forcing — the New Minor Forcing Convention. When responder has a poor hand, the auction would be propelled to too high a level. So, how does responder "get out" in his minor suit? How can responder tell opener he has a longer minor suit he would rather use as trumps, than play in a notrump contract? By use of the "Funny Jump."

When the auction proceeds

NORTH	EAST	SOUTH	WEST
1 minor	Pass	1 major	Pass
1 Notrump	Pass	3 unbid minor	

the message responder is sending is:

1) I have a 4-card major

2) I have a 6-card minor

3) I have less (6 to 9 HCP) than invitational values

Typical hands would be

♠ 8	♠ 82
♥ J842	♥ KQ63
♦ KQJ832	♦ J97542
♣ 62	♣ Q

In most situations, responder's jump to three of a minor will end the auction. Opener will always have at least a doubleton in responder's minor suit, and will not have a reason to remove the contract to a different level or strain.

The "Funny Jump" Convention is not available <u>except</u> over opener's One Notrump rebid. If opener rebids One Spade instead of One Notrump, responder's jump to three of the unbid minor does not show the weak 4-6 hand. Rather, it shows an invitational 5-5 hand, such as

♠ 92
♥ KJ1084
♦ AJ942
♣ Q

Some partnership play this sequence as showing spade support, game-forcing values, and a singleton or void in the diamond suit — a "splinter." A typical hand would be

♠ Q832
♥ KJ963
♦ 2
♣ AK4

And, if over the One Notrump rebid, responder jumps in opener's minor suit, rather than in the unbid one, he is showing a hand with invitational (9 to 11 HCP) values, and, of course, four hearts or spades but also five-card support for opener's minor suit. In the auction of

NORTH	EAST	SOUTH	WEST
1♣	Pass	1♠	Pass
1NT	Pass	3♣	

responder could have

♠ QJ42
♥ A4
♦ 82
♣ KJ1083

or

♠ J842
♥ A4
♦ J
♣ KQ9832

WEAK JUMP SHIFTS

In Standard methods, when responder makes a jump shift bid, such as

NORTH	EAST	SOUTH	WEST
1♦	Pass	2♠	

it shows a hand with interest in exploring a slam contract, usually either in opener's suit, responder's suit or Notrump.

But, playing two-over-one, we can make a simple or non-jump bid in a lower ranking suit if we want to show a hand of at least game-going strength. And, if we bid a high-ranking suit at the one-level, there are enough gadgets at our disposal in the later stages of the auction to show interest in slam.

Therefore, a jump-shift in a higher-ranking suit shows a hand that did not have enough values to legitimately respond (less than 6 HCP) and a long suit. A typical hand we would have to make a weak jump shift in spades over partner's opening bid of One Diamond would be

♠ J108642
♥ 82
♦ Q43
♣ J7

If we had

♠ K108642
♥ 82
♦ Q43
♣ J7

we would respond One Spade to partner's One Diamond Opening.

A jump shift in a lower-ranking suit would show invitational values (See *INVITATIONAL JUMPS*). If we had a long lower-ranking suit and insufficient values to respond to partner's opening bid, we would pass, or start with a bid of One Forcing Notrump (if our partner's opening bid was in a major suit).

In addition to the obvious descriptive nature of the weak jump shift bid, an extremely important advantage of the convention is that it makes it much more difficult for the opponents to enter the bidding with marginal values. For example, if the bidding proceeds

NORTH	EAST	SOUTH	WEST
1♦	Pass	2♠	?

what does West bid with each of the following hands:

♠ Q4	♠ 1086
♥ KJ83	♥ AQJ83
♦ A4	♦ Q4
♣ J742	♣ KJ2

In keeping with this pre-emptive nature of the weak jump shift, opener's rebids are consistently obstructive with weak hands and constructive with strong hands. A simple raise is preemptive and totally non-forcing:

NORTH	EAST	SOUTH	WEST
1♣	Pass	2♥	Pass
3♥			

A new suit should be forcing and show an extremely good hand, such as

♠ A4
♥ K
♦ AQJ94
♣ KQJ83

would be a typical hand for the auction of

NORTH	EAST	SOUTH	WEST
1♦	Pass	2♥	Pass
3♣			

Two Notrump implies a fit and requests more information from responder about the quality of his hand and his suit. "Ogust" responses can be given to disclose the requested information. Responder in the auction of

NORTH	EAST	SOUTH	WEST
1♦	Pass	2♥	Pass
2NT	Pass	?	

would bid

Three Clubs with a bad suit and bad hand
Three Diamonds with a good suit and bad hand
Three Hearts with a bad suit and good hand
Three Spades with a good suit and good hand.

Remember that "good" and "bad" are descriptive terms within the context of limits that are very small. That is, the high card point value of the hand is five or less and the suit is usually five to seven cards long. So

♠ 8
♥ K109863
♦ J4
♣ J987

would certainly be described as a "good" hand, and, may even be considered to contain a "good" suit.

A typical hand for opener to bid Two Notrump over partner's weak jump shift is

♠ KQ
♥ QJ
♦ AK632
♣ A1062

SPLINTERS

An unusual jump in an unbid suit signifies shortness (a singleton or void) in the suit bid, a fit for the implied trump suit, and game-going values. In other words, in Standard bidding, the auction of

NORTH	EAST	SOUTH	WEST
1♠	Pass	4♦	

shows a singleton or void in diamonds a spade fit (4 or 5 cards) for partner, and enough values to force to game (about 10 - 13 HCP).

Similarly, the auction of

NORTH	EAST	SOUTH	WEST
1♣	Pass	1♠	Pass
4♦			

shows a singleton or void in diamonds, a four-card spade fit for partner, and enough values to force to game (19 or more points).

A more sophisticated treatment used by some experts is to play a Three Diamond bid here to show a singleton diamond and a Four Diamond bid to show a void. In both cases, opener must have enough values (19 points) to force to game opposite responder's minimum One Spade response.

Employing Standard methods, the auction of

NORTH	EAST	SOUTH	WEST
1♠	Pass	2♥	Pass
4♦			

shows a singleton or a void in diamonds, a heart fit and enough values to force to game (16 or more points). The 16-point figure is determined by the fact that responder must have at least 10 points to make a two-over-one bid within the Standard bidding framework.

When the partnership is using the two-over-one game force system, the requirements for responder's Two Heart bid have increased to game-going strength (12 or more points). Therefore, the strength requirement for opener's splinter bid of Four Diamonds is lessened to a mere 13 points (a relatively minimum opener). Opener still promises a heart fit and shortness in diamonds. But responder should not expect any extra strength. As a matter of fact, opener is unlikely to have an interest in a slam since the Four Diamond bid takes up any exploratory room for slam investigation. If opener has a hand such as

> ♠ AJ872
> ♥ KQ54
> ♦ 6
> ♣ AQ4

he should bid Three Hearts and await developments. Perhaps he will get an opportunity to show his diamond shortness later.

A hand with which he would bid Four Diamonds immediately is

> ♠ A9632
> ♥ KQ52
> ♦ 6
> ♣ KJ4

Making the cheapest possible bid (two-over-one) in a lower-ranking suit commits the partnership to a game contract. Bidding a Forcing Notrump, then cheaply bidding a new suit shows a very weak hand with unbalanced distribution. So what does responder do when he has an unbalanced hand — one long suit — and invitational values of 9 to 11 HCP?

Early proponents of the two-over-one system and some current experts bid and rebid their suit, cancelling the message that the partnership has enough values to bid to a game-level contract. These partnerships would play that

NORTH	EAST	SOUTH	WEST
1♥	Pass	2♣	Pass
2♦	Pass	3♣	

or

NORTH	EAST	SOUTH	WEST
1♥	1♠	2♣	Pass
2NT	Pass	3♣	

would be non-forcing and show a six-card club suit and 9 to 11 HCP, much like the "off-in-competition" pairs would bid.

This method is not recommended because, particularly in competitive auctions, opener would be forced to make exact value-showing bids too early in the auction. With

♠ K103
♥ KQJ84
♦ KJ
♣ K62

should opener bid Two Notrump or Three Notrump or Three Clubs in the auction

NORTH	EAST	SOUTH	WEST
1♥	1♠	2♣	Pass
?			

Should opener bid Two or Three Hearts with

♠ K103
♥ AQJ1082
♦ KJ83
♣ K

in the auction above?

Should opener double or bid Five Clubs with

♠ A82
♥ KQJ63
♦ AJ
♣ KJ4

in the auction

NORTH	EAST	SOUTH	WEST
1♥	1♠	2♣	3♠
?			

The answers to all these dilemmas are determined by which "system" the partnership is using. Could responder have only 9 to 11 HCP or is he guaranteeing at least 12 or more HCP?

To avoid these problems **Invitational Jumps** are employed. When responder holds a six-card or longer suit that is lower-ranking than opener's and has invitational values, he jumps to the three level in his own suit:

109

NORTH	EAST	SOUTH	WEST
1♠	Pass	3♦	

or

NORTH	EAST	SOUTH	WEST
1♠	2♣	3♦	

Note that these jumps are used in or out of competition. If the partnership is playing two-over-one **off** in competition, the difference between bidding and rebidding responder's suit at the two, and, then the three level and making an immediate jump to the three level is in the quality of the suit. The bid of two, and, then, three would tend to show a broken suit, more favorable to a suit contract than to a notrump contract. The immediate jump to the three level shows a more-or-less solid or "one-loser" suit, **invitational** to **three notrump.** The contrasting hands might be

♠ Q
♥ A62
♦ KJ10832
♣ J32

and

♠ Q
♥ Q62
♦ AQJ1083
♣ 432

Note that neither hand has a fit for partner's suit.

In the auction of

NORTH	EAST	SOUTH	WEST
1♥	Pass	3♣	

opener's responsibilities following his partner's invitational jump are usually

110

1) to bid Three Notrump if possible:

♠ QJ7
♥ KJ842
♦ A32
♣ K4

2) to pass with a minimum hand and no better place to play the hand:

♠ QJ6
♥ AJ862
♦ KJ9
♣ 95

3) to rebid his own suit with a minimum and a suit that is probably better than his partner's:

♠ Q4
♥ KQJ986
♦ A42
♣ J4

4) to bid a new suit (forcing) with a good hand that is either too strong for Three Notrump or too unbalanced.

♠ AK
♥ KQ1083
♦ AQJ4
♣ J2

Those who do not elect to use *INVITATIONAL JUMPS* to describe a hand with 9 to 11 points and a six-card suit must begin by responding with a forcing notrump. After opener rebids, responder shows his invitational values by bidding his suit at the three level. This second bid by responder will often be a jump bid.

NORTH	EAST	SOUTH	WEST
1♠	Pass	1NT	Pass
2♣	Pass	3♦ or 3♥	

NEW MINOR FORCING

Because all jumps are either invitational or non-forcing after opener's One Notrump rebid, a method of creating a forcing bidding sequence is needed. The **New Minor Forcing** (NMF) convention fills that need. Its two primary functions are:

1. To search for the "golden fit" of eight cards in a major suit.

2. To build a forcing auction while showing a minor-suit trump fit.

We will demonstrate both uses in this section.

When responder has a five-card major and a hand whose strength is invitational or better, he becomes very interested in determining whether or not opener has three-card support for his major suit — establishing the "golden fit" of eight cards. The New Minor Forcing convention is a method of asking opener the question "How many cards do you hold in my major suit?" It is a **convention** because it uses bids that do not necessarily show suits or values that they appear to show. In other words, when responder bids Two Diamonds in certain auctions, he is not promising that he has length in the diamond suit — he may have a singleton or a void.

It is important to remember that the New Minor Forcing convention comes into use **only** in specific situations. In order for it to be operative, the following conditions must exist:

1) Responder must have bid one of a major suit over opener's opening one bid;

2) Opener must have rebid One Notrump

or

Opener may have jump rebid Two Notrump.

Auctions such as

NORTH	EAST	SOUTH	WEST
1♦	Pass	1♠	P
1NT			

or

NORTH	EAST	SOUTH	WEST
1♣	Pass	1♠	P
2NT			

are fertile ground for implementation of the New Minor Forcing convention. Although the requirements cited above are necessary before NMF can be employed, it is not employed every time those conditions exist. When is NMF employed? It should be used whenever

1) Responder has invitational or better (10 HCP) values and

2) There is a potential 8-card major suit fit **or** responder has interest in establishing a minor suit fit.

These two requirements need some elaboration. First, responder must have at least invitational values. When responder has a weak hand (9 or fewer HCP), he is forced to make a more unilateral decision regarding finalizing the strain and the level of the contract. Usually he either passes the One Notrump bid with a relatively flat hand, bids two of his suit to end the auction, or bids two of his partner's original suit to end the auction.

With

> ♠ Q4
> ♥ QJ863
> ♦ 832
> ♣ K74

in the auction of

NORTH	EAST	SOUTH	WEST
1♣	Pass	1♥	Pass
1NT			

he would pass One Notrump or bid Two Hearts. It would be nice to know whether or not opener has three hearts. But the investigation would risk catapulting the partnership to danger-ous heights, as we shall see later. Responder's hand is relatively flat and should support a notrump contract nicely, even if opener has three hearts. And, if responder elects to bid Two Hearts, he is guaranteed a seven-card fit. The point is: Although responder would like to ask the opener the question "Do you have three Hearts?", he can't afford to do so with such meager values. Responder must make his best "guess" at a final contract.

With

♠ J4
♥ K9863
♦ J2
♣ QJ82

responder would rebid Two Clubs. It's true that opener may have only three clubs and the contract would be played in a 4-3 fit. However, there are many advantages to the Two Club bid. Opener may have five clubs. Opener may have three hearts and bid Two Hearts, especially in matchpoint contests. Opener may have neither of those features, but be relatively wide-open in the spade suit. A suit contract would be superior to a notrump contract in that case, even if the suit contract were only a 4-3 fit. Opener could have

♠ AQ3
♥ QJ4
♦ 1053
♣ K1094

With

♠ Q2
♥ A98632
♦ 1032
♣ J6

responder would rebid Two Hearts. He has found the "golden fit" of eight cards.

With

♠ 2
♥ K8632
♦ QJ432
♣ J7

responder would rebid Two Hearts. Here, we may not have found the eight-card fit. But notrump is out of the question. And bidding Two Diamonds would be forcing and show invitational values. Bidding Three Diamonds would be a "Funny Jump" (see *FUNNY JUMPS*) and would show a 4-6 pattern. So responder's safest refuge is at the two level with hearts as trumps.

How should opener respond to the New Minor Forcing convention? He is being asked a specific question: Do you have three-card support for my suit? If the answer is "yes," he should bid responder's major suit. If he has a minimum hand, he takes a simple preference:

NORTH	EAST	SOUTH	WEST
1♣	Pass	1♠	Pass
1NT	Pass	2♦	Pass
2♠			

If he has a maximum hand, he should jump the bidding

NORTH	EAST	SOUTH	WEST
1♣	Pass	1♠	Pass
1NT	Pass	2♦	Pass
3♠			

Note that "minimum" and "maximum" are terms used within the context of the 12 to 15 HCP range of the One Notrump rebid. There are some response systems in use which show or deny major honor cards or show opener's hand pattern in the major suit as well as show the maximum hand, but they are not discussed here.

Opener's options are relatively few when answering "yes" to responder's question about support for his suit. When the answer is "no," there are more options, making judgement come into play to a greater extent. When opener does not have three-card support for responder's major, he has an opportunity to further describe his hand. Priorities of description are:

1) Show four cards in the other major suit;
2) Show extra length in opener's minor suit;
3) Show four cards in the "new" minor suit;
4) Show a minimum or maximum hand.

Let's look at these options when the auction has proceeded

NORTH	EAST	SOUTH	WEST
1♦	Pass	1♠	Pass
1NT	Pass	2♣	Pass
?			

Of course, with three-card spade support, opener would bid either Two or Three Spades.

Without three spades, opener would bid hearts if he held four of them; he would bid Two Hearts with a minimum hand or Three

Hearts with a maximum hand. Or, depending on partnership style, he would bid Two Hearts with all hands containing four hearts. Opener would also bid Two Diamonds to deny three spades and show five or six-card diamond length. Some partnerships do not want to use valuable bidding room here when the pair is committed to bidding to a higher level.

Let's digress slightly from our examination of opener's "no" responses to make a valuable point concerning the "forcing" nature of the New Minor Forcing convention. Often the question is asked "I know that the bid of the new minor suit is forcing but **forcing to what?**" Here's the answer: The bid of the new minor suit in applicable auctions is forcing to:

    A) Two Notrump
    B) Three of a major suit
    C) Four of a minor suit

except

when opener rebids Two of responder's major suit, to show three-card support and a **minimum** hand (**minimum** because he did not jump to Three), responder may pass with values insufficient to drive to a game opposite that minimum opening hand.

and

When responder rebids his major suit at the cheapest (two) level after opener shows a minimum hand without three-card support such as

NORTH	EAST	SOUTH	WEST
1♦	Pass	1♠	Pass
1NT	Pass	2♣	Pass
2♦	Pass	2♠	

This is why responder needs at least 9 HCP to use NMF — because it forces the partnership to the bidding level cited above.

There is great comfort and utility in knowing the bidding can not stop until a definite level is reached. A good example occurs when responder has a game forcing hand with a fit for partner's minor suit. With responder's hand of

♠ Q4
♥ KQ83
♦ A2
♣ KQ762

the auction may proceed

NORTH	EAST	SOUTH	WEST
1♣	Pass	1♥	Pass
1NT	Pass	2♦	Pass
2♥, 2♠ or 2NT	Pass	3♣	

Three clubs is a forcing bid, shows at least 9 HCP, an unbalanced hand with a minimum of four and, more likely, five clubs. It is certainly helpful that responder does not have to jump the bidding beyond three notrump in order to show a fit for partner's minor suit and a hand that is strong enough to force opener through at least one more round of bidding.

Note: Some partnerships have agreed that, when NMF is employed, and responder raises opener's minor suit at his first opportunity after NMF, a **game**-level contract must be reached. Therefore, responder would need at least 12 HCP to produce the example auction. Other partnerships play that a level of bidding described earlier (Two Notrump, Three of a major suit [with exceptions noted above], Four of a minor suit) is the demanded limit of bidding.

Let's return to our discussion of opener's priorities when he does not have three-card support for responder's major suit. We've already seen that he may show four cards in the other major suit by bidding it. A jump in the unbid major would show four cards and a maximum in some partnerships.

Without the ability to bid a major suit, opener may be able to show extra length (five or more) in the minor suit he originally bid. For example:

NORTH	EAST	SOUTH	WEST
1♦	Pass	1♥	Pass
1NT	Pass	2♣	Pass
2♦			

or

NORTH	EAST	SOUTH	WEST
1♣	Pass	1♠	P
1NT	Pass	2♦	P
3♣			

Or he may be able to show a four-card fit for the "new minor" by raising the bidding in that suit:

NORTH	EAST	SOUTH	WEST
1♦	Pass	1♥	Pass
1NT	Pass	2♣	Pass
3♣			

Opener would have 2-2-5-4 or 3-2-4-4 shape to make the Three Club bid. However, if he had either of those two distributions, he may elect to bid Two Notrump rather than raise the level of bidding to the three level in a suit that is probably "artificial." How does opener decide whether to bid Two Notrump or to raise the new minor suit? The partnership should adopt the style of bidding Two Notrump with minimum hands and raising the minor suit with a maximum. This is a good way to convey a significant amount of information without using much bidding space.

DRURY

Opening bids in third seat may be made with less values than would be required to open the bidding in first or second seat. So when responder chooses a response to the third seat opener, he does not want to propel the partnership to the three level when opener's values were shaded. Hence, the Drury Convention is employed. It was conceived so responder could ask a third-seat opener "Do you have a "real" opener, or do you have fewer values than you would normally have to open the bidding in first or second seat?" Since its inception, the use of the convention has been extended so responder can ask a fourth-seat opener the same question.

When the Drury convention was originated, it was not necessary for responder to possess a fit for opener's suit in order to request a clarification of opener's values. But, over time, the requirement that responder must have at least a three-card fit for opener's major suit opening-bid suit has evolved.

Responder must also possess sufficient values to invite a game bid in the partnership's major suit. That is, he must hold limit-raise values of nine or more points.

The way responder activates the Drury convention is by bidding Two Clubs in response to opener's third or fourth-seat opening bid of One Spade or One Heart. For example

NORTH	EAST	SOUTH	WEST
		Pass	Pass
1♥	Pass	2♣	

or

NORTH	EAST	SOUTH	WEST
		Pass	Pass
1♥	Double	2♣	

or

NORTH	EAST	SOUTH	WEST
		Pass	Pass
1♥	1♠	2♣	

Some parterships use a Two Club bid over the opponent's One Notrump overcall as a Drury bid. Others do not.

Opener's responses to the Drury inquiry are structured. Originally, a Two Diamond bid told responder that opener did not have enough values to open the bidding in first or second seat. Some partnerships still employ this method. Rebidding opener's suit shows a "real" opening bid, but nothing extra. Bids other than Two Diamonds are help-suit game tries or short-suit game tries by partnership preference and agreement.

More partnerships today use **Reverse** Drury than use original Drury. Opener's responses using Reverse Drury are "opposite" from his responses using original Drury. A two Diamond bid shows more than a minimum hand; a hand that would accept some but, perhaps, not all, game tries. A rebid of opener's suit shows a sub-standard hand; one that would not accept any game try.

An auction of

NORTH	EAST	SOUTH	WEST
		Pass	Pass
1♠	Pass	2♣	Pass
2♠			

would rarely produce any bid by responder other than Pass. A suit bid here would show a super-maximum hand and would be a help-suit game try.

121

The auction of

NORTH	EAST	SOUTH	WEST
		Pass	Pass
1♥	Pass	2♣	Pass
2♠			

invites responder to make a help-suit game try. If it is the right suit, opener may jump to game. For example, with

> ♠ KJ832
> ♥ K87
> ♦ AJ
> ♣ Q42

opener would bid Four Spades in the auction

NORTH	EAST	SOUTH	WEST
		Pass	Pass
1♠	Pass	2♣	Pass
2♦	Pass	3♣	

but would bid Three Hearts with

> ♠ KJ832
> ♥ J1042
> ♦ A4
> ♣ K8

Sometimes opener appears to be making a help-suit game try and showing a good hand by bidding a new suit over Two Clubs:

NORTH	EAST	SOUTH	WEST
		Pass	Pass
1♠	Pass	2♣	Pass
2♥			

But, when he jumps to a game-level bid over responder's sign-off, he is showing an interest in bidding a slam.

NORTH	EAST	SOUTH	WEST
		Pass	Pass
1♠	Pass	2♣	Pass
2♥	Pass	2♠	Pass
4♠			

An important aspect of the Drury or Reverse Drury convention is that, when it could be invoked and is not, bids by a passed hand that would normally show a fit for opener's major suit no longer show the values or the support they did as an unpassed hand. Examples of this principle are the Two Notrump bid, the Three Club response, and the jump raise.

Since responder bids Two Clubs with all hands that contain a limit raise in the auction of

NORTH	EAST	SOUTH	WEST
		Pass	Pass
1♥	Pass	?	

a bid of Two Notrump can no longer show a fit for opener's major. What does it show? It shows both minor suits with invitational values. A typical hand would be

♠ Q2
♥ J
♦ KJ842
♣ A9763

A jump raise would show a fit, but insufficient values to make a simple raise — less than six points. A typical hand would be

♠ 4
♥ J863
♦ Q9742
♣ Q65

A jump to Three Clubs is necessary when responder has a long club suit and invitational values (9 to 11 points). Responder cannot bid Two Clubs since that would show a limit raise for opener's major suit.

♠ J4
♥ K9
♦ 763
♣ AQ10973

Playing Pre-emptive Jump Raises in Competition, a cue bid would serve to show a limit raise in the auction of

NORTH	EAST	SOUTH	WEST
		Pass	Pass
1♥	2♦	3♦	

There are many additional nuances and understandings which good partnerships incorporate into their passed hand major suit raise structure. but Drury or Reverse Drury is the cornerstone of all such structures.

INVERTED MINORS

Standard methods do not provide a conventional way of describing responder's hand which has game-forcing values and a fit for opener's minor suit. Delayed jumps after two-over-ones or applications of the New Minor Forcing or Fourth Suit Forcing conventions enable responder to tell opener he has such a hand. But these tactics often require responder to start the auction by bidding a "phony" suit. For example, playing Standard methods which include limit raises, what should responder's bid be when opener starts the bidding with One Diamond:

♠ KJ4	♠ QJ	♠ A43	♠ J2
♥ A2	♥ K52	♥ 98	♥ Q2
♦ AK83	♦ QJ1083	♦ AQJ9	♦ KQJ1086
♣ K632	♣ A42	♣ Q874	♣ AQ3

In all of these cases, Two Clubs is probably the "correct" bid, although it hardly gives opener an accurate picture of responder's hand early in the auction. Opener may raise clubs. Is Three Diamonds now by responder forcing? What if opener rebids Two Notrump? Is Three Diamonds non-forcing?

To avoid such dilemmas, the Inverted Minor convention is employed. In its simplest form it can be explained by stating that jump raises show weak hands (5 to 9 points, five-card support) and simple raises show better hands (10 or more points, five-card support). In rare instances, responder may have only four-card support when making a strong raise. In the context of the two-over-one system, an additional requirement is that responder can not have a four-card major suit. Otherwise, he would bid it or make a negative double. There is one exception: When responder has only one four-card major and a negative double would show both majors, he may elect to raise opener's minor suit rather that bid his one four-card major suit at the two level. The auctions would be

125

NORTH	EAST	SOUTH	WEST
1♦	2♣	?	

or

NORTH	EAST	SOUTH	WEST
1♣	2♦	?	

In the first auction with

♠ AQ42
♥ Q4
♦ KJ832
♣ Q3

responder would probably bid Two Diamonds.

In the second auction with

♠ 32
♥ KQ42
♦ J4
♣ QJ1042

responder would probably bid Three Clubs. Some partnerships play that a negative double in these auctions does not promise both major suits, merely one major suit and a fit for partner's minor or both majors without a fit. But this treatment should not be tested in unpracticed partnerships.

In the auctions where the minor suit is simply raised to show at least 10 points, since the eight-card major suit fit has been eliminated as a likely possibility (opener may have a six-card minor suit and a five-card major suit) the priorities revert to

1) Explore the possibility of a notrump contract.
2) Play in a minor suit.

Therefore, opener's rebids are structured to facilitate exploration of notrump possibilities. With both major suits stopped and at least a doubleton in the other minor suit, opener rebids an appropriate number of Notrump determined by the strength of his hand. With a minimum of 12 to 14 HCP, he rebids Two Notrump. With 15 to 17 points he bids a new suit. You may ask why he didn't open the bidding with One Notrump if he has 15 to 17 HCP and a relatively flat hand. With

♠ AK63
♥ K2
♦ KQJ62
♣ 87

the opening bid of One Notrump is not recommended. But now that opener knows a major-suit fit does not exist, three notrump is the most likely final contract and the best bid with the hand shown.

With 18 or 19 HCP and flat distribution, he rebids Three Notrump.

With an unbalanced hand, or a hand that does not have both major suits stopped, opener "approaches" notrump by beginning to bid his "stoppers." With

♠ 832
♥ KJ4
♦ AQJ6
♣ J32

the auction would proceed

NORTH	EAST	SOUTH	WEST
1♦	Pass	2♦	Pass
2♥			

127

Superficially this shows a hand of unknown strength with hearts but not spades stopped. But it could be a non-minimum unbalanced hand such as

♠ 4
♥ KQ42
♦ AQJ63
♣ KJ4

Based on frequency, responder should rebid assuming opener has the minimum hand with hearts but not spades stopped. So with spades and clubs "stopped" and a minimum inverted raise, responder should rebid Two Notrump in the auction of

NORTH	EAST	SOUTH	WEST
1♦	Pass	2♦	Pass
2♥	Pass	?	

A typical hand for this bidding would be

♠ K32
♥ Q2
♦ Q5432
♣ QJ2

Opener can bid appropriately afterwards based on responder's accurate description of his hand.

With 18 or 19 HCP and a flat hand such as

♠ KJ2
♥ AQ4
♦ AQJ2
♣ Q32

Opener would rebid Three Notrump

With spades stopped but not clubs, and with any strength hand, responder should rebid Two Spades in the example auction. His hand could be

♠ KJ2
♥ A2
♦ Q8754
♣ 642

or

♠ KQ4
♥ A2
♦ KQJ63
♣ 642

Opener should continue his approach bidding on the next round. If he is still hesitant to bid Notrump, He should retreat to the safety of his partnership's minor suit. With

♠ Q9
♥ KQ42
♦ AQ32
♣ 832

in the auction of

NORTH	EAST	SOUTH	WEST
1♦	Pass	2♦	Pass
2♥	Pass	2♠	Pass

opener should bid Three Diamonds. This bid says "I have a minimum-strength hand and I don't like a Notrump contract because I'm afraid we don't have clubs well stopped." One of responder's appropriate bids might be "Pass." With

♠ KJ4
♥ A3
♦ K8764
♣ 976

responder should see no future in bidding beyond Three Diamonds.

Another weapon in the arsenal of partnerships which play the Inverted Minor convention is the Splinter Bid. Unusual jumps show singletons or voids in the suit bid. The auction of

NORTH	EAST	SOUTH	WEST
1♦	Pass	2♦	Pass
3♠			

and

NORTH	EAST	SOUTH	WEST
1♦	Pass	2♦	Pass
2♥	Pass	3♠	

show short spade suits with sufficient values to force to at least a game contract opposite minimum values guaranteed by partner. An interest in bidding a slam is definitely present.

Once responder has made a pre-emptive jump raise in opener's minor suit, he is usually finished bidding unless opener shows exceptional strength. Auctions such as

NORTH	EAST	SOUTH	WEST
1♣	Pass	3♣	Pass
3NT			

or

NORTH	EAST	SOUTH	WEST
1♣	Pass	3♣	Pass
4♣			

do not invite responder to bid again. It would take a highly unusual hand such as

♠ 2
♥ 6
♦ QJ93
♣ KJ98632

to give responder license to bid again opposite opener's non-forcing auction.

If opener has a very strong hand he may initiate questions in order to solicit a clearer description of responder's hand. Usually these questions are pointed toward finding a notrump contract. The sequence

NORTH	EAST	SOUTH	WEST
1♦	Pass	3♦	Pass
3♥			

is asking responder to bid Three Notrump if he has the spade suit stopped. Here again, the club suit is tacitly "stopped" because the assumption is that, if responder does not have a four-card major suit, he must have some length in the other minor suit.

If opener bids a new suit at the four level, thereby preventing a Three Notrump bid, it is a cue bid or a splinter bid, investigating a game or a slam contract. For example

NORTH	EAST	SOUTH	WEST
1♦	Pass	3♦	Pass
4♣			

asks responder to re-evaluate his hand with the knowledge that opener has values in the club suit. It is a "help suit game try." And

NORTH	EAST	SOUTH	WEST
1♦	Pass	3♦	Pass
4♠			

is a "splinter bid," forcing the partnership to bid to at least the game level and inviting responder to cue bid an Ace so the partnership can bid a slam. With

♠ 83
♥ K2
♦ J10876
♣ A432

the auction should proceed

NORTH	EAST	SOUTH	WEST
1♦	Pass	3♦	Pass
4♠	Pass	5♣	

Each partnership should decide whether or not to use the Inverted Minor convention "on" or "off" in competition. The discussions above assume the partnership was playing the convention "on" in competition. But some players prefer to revert to Standard methods if the opponents overall. That is, a simple raise shows a weak (6 to 9 points) hand and is non-forcing. A jump raise is a limit raise (10 to 12 points) and a cue bid shows a game forcing hand (12 or more points) with a fit.

Over opponents' takeout doubles, the Flip Flop Convention is employed. The name "Flip Flop" comes from the fact that the values shown are opposite from the values shown by the same bids if major suits are involved. The auction of

NORTH	EAST	SOUTH	WEST
1♣	Double	2 Notrump	

shows a pre-emptive raise of 6 to 9 points and five or more clubs. The auction of

NORTH	EAST	SOUTH	WEST
1♣	Double	3♣	

shows a limit raise of 10 to 12 points and five or more clubs. With five or more clubs and a forcing raise of 12 or more points, "Redouble" is the appropriate first bid by responder.

A primary advantage of the Flip Flop convention is that, if a Three Notrump contract is reached after responder shows invitational values, the opponent who has the strong hand (the "doubler") will be on lead, forced to lead away from his honor cards.

SUPPORT DOUBLES

Opener must have a five-card suit to open the bidding with a bid of One Heart or One Spade. So when he opens with One Club or One Diamond, he may have four hearts and/or four spades. Responder dutifully bids his four-card major and opener raises the major suit to show four-card support. Thus the "Golden Fit" of eight cards is found.

This scenario applies in a competitive auction. In the auction of

NORTH	EAST	SOUTH	WEST
1♣	Pass	1♥	2♦
2♥			

the Two Heart bid shows four-card support.

"Support Doubles" enable opener to show three-card support by doubling the opponent's overcall. Here "double" says nothing about opener's desire to penalize the opponents. It merely says "I have exactly three cards in the suit you bid, Partner." Opener may have a good hand or a bad hand. He may have a three-card club suit or a seven-card club suit. He may have diamonds stopped for notrump or he may not. He is merely communicating the fact that he possesses exactly three hearts.

The knowledge that opener has exactly three-card support for responder's major suit is particularly valuable when responder has at least five cards in the suit. It enables him to compete or to bid freely knowing the partnership has an eight-card major suit fit. Without support doubles, opener may raise with only three-card support, especially in competition. So responder must bid "in the dark" in auctions such as

NORTH	EAST	SOUTH	WEST
1♣	Pass	1♥	2♦
2♥	3♦	?	

with

♠ A8
♥ Q832
♦ KJ4
♣ 8432

should responder bid Three Hearts, Double, or bid Three Notrump? If responder knew opener had four hearts, he would not consider doing anything other than bidding more hearts.

When responder has shown a five-card suit, support doubles do not apply. In the auction of

NORTH	EAST	SOUTH	WEST
1♣	1♥	1♠	

responder shows at least five spades. Therefore, if opener has three spades or four spades the auction will continue

NORTH	EAST	SOUTH	WEST
1♣	1♥	1♠	2♥
2♠			

"Double" by North would be a co-operative penalty double and would imply fewer than three spades.

WALSH FRAGMENTS

A hand is valuable not only if it possesses many high card points, but also if it has shape — long suits and short suits which enhance trick taking potential. When opener starts the bidding with One Club or One Diamond, responder bids One Heart or One Spade and opener has four-card support for responder's major, the value of opener's hand has increased. And, when opener has 6-4 shape, he has extra trick-taking potential, since his long suit can eventually be developed to provide a parking place for responder's losers. Armed with this information, responder may elect to pursue a slam contract with marginal values.

Opener tells responder he has the 6-4 shape by jumping to the four level in his minor suit at his first opportunity. For example

NORTH	EAST	SOUTH	WEST
1♣	Pass	1♠	Pass
4♣			

or

NORTH	EAST	SOUTH	WEST
1♦	Pass	1♥	1♠
4♦			

shows a six-card minor suit and a four-card fit for responder's major suit. Opener should not have a minimum hand and should not have a very strong hand. Therefore, his range should be about 14 to 17 HCP.

When responder has shown a five-card major suit by bidding over interference, such as

NORTH	EAST	SOUTH	WEST
1♦	1♥	1♠	

opener may have a 6-3 shape to make a Walsh Fragment jump.

Armed with this information, responder would explore a slam by cue-bidding if convenient, or asking for Aces, even with somewhat minimum values but some controls. For example, with

♠ KQ82
♥ 832
♦ A4
♣ J962

after the auction of

NORTH	EAST	SOUTH	WEST
1♣	Pass	1♠	Pass
4♣	Pass	?	

responder should cue-bid Four Diamonds. His four-card club fit indicates slam is possible if the partnership can stop the initial red-suit attack by the opponents. Opposite

♠ A976
♥ A4
♦ 8
♣ AK10754

a spade grand slam is dependent upon bringing spades and clubs home with no losers. The slam has about a 70% chance of success, although the partnership has only twenty-five HCP. If there is a black suit loser, it takes a heart lead to defeat a small slam.

NEGATIVE DOUBLES

The two-over-one system utilizes negative doubles in the traditional manner. "Double" is used to "bid" a suit when it is too short to bid outright or when responder's hand is too weak to show such strength. For example, in the auction

NORTH	EAST	SOUTH
1♦	1♥	Double

responder is showing exactly four spades. If he had five spades he could bid One Spade rather than Double.

Note: Some partnerships play that "Double" here shows fewer than four spades and One Spade shows four or more.

The reason these partnerships choose to deny four spades when they make a negative double is that there are hands with which responder wants to enter the auction, but does not have four spades or sufficient values to make a two-over-one. For example:

♠ QJ2
♥ 94
♦ K83
♣ QJ1065

If a negative double promised four spades, responder would have to pass.

Returning to our discussion of traditional negative doubles, with

♠ J82
♥ Q
♦ KJ9763
♣ J42

the auction would proceed

NORTH	EAST	SOUTH	WEST
1♥	1♠	Double	

Responder would like to bid diamonds, but lacks the strength to go to the two level, since such a bid promises 10 points in Standard methods. If he makes a negative double and follows that bid with the bid of a new suit, the sequence shows a long suit and a weak hand.

The principles are the same utilizing the two-over-one system except, since the strength required to make a two-over-one bid is 12 or more points, negative doubles must be employed with hands that extend to the 10 to 11 point range. In Standard methods, responder would bid his suit directly with these hands.

Direct jumps in lower-ranking suits are invitational, showing semi-solid suits. (See *INVITATIONAL JUMPS*). In the auction of

NORTH	EAST	SOUTH	WEST
1♥	1♠	3♣	

a typical hand for the auction would be

♠ J6
♥ 43
♦ K62
♣ AQJ842

A negative double followed by a jump is invitational, with a broken suit. For example

NORTH	EAST	SOUTH	WEST
1♥	1♠	Double	Pass
2♣	Pass	3♦	

would show a hand such as

♠ Q8
♥ 42
♦ KJ10832
♣ AJ5

When the partnership adopts the approach that two-over-one is "Off in Competition," things become much more complicated.

When responder's two-over-one bid is not forcing to game, a negative double is less likely to show a suit longer than four cards. For example, playing two-over-one on in competition, with

♠ J4
♥ KJ1083
♦ 842
♣ KJ8

in the auction of

NORTH	EAST	SOUTH	WEST
1♠	2♣	?	

"Double" is the appropriate bid, showing at least four hearts and at least eight points.

But, playing two-over-one **off** in competition, the hand shown above would bid Two Hearts. Therefore, playing two-over-one

off in competition, "Double" would tend to show exactly four hearts, since the eight point hand that is required to make either bid would bid Two Hearts if it had five hearts.

Some players require less strength to make a negative double and more strength to make a two-over-one, even **off** in competition. But whatever your agreements are, you will find yourself making more negative doubles if you play two-over-one **on** in competition than if you play it **off** in competition.

50 HIGHLY-RECOMMENDED TITLES

CALL TOLL FREE 1-800-274-2221
IN THE U.S. & CANADA TO ORDER ANY OF
THEM OR TO REQUEST OUR
FULL-COLOR 64 PAGE CATALOG OF
ALL BRIDGE BOOKS IN PRINT,
SUPPLIES AND GIFTS.

FOR BEGINNERS
#0300 Future Champions' Bridge Series 9.95
#2130 Kantar-Introduction to Declarer's Play 10.00
#2135 Kantar-Introduction to Defender's Play 10.00
#0101 Stewart-Baron-The Bridge Book 1 .... 9.95
#1121 Silverman-Elementary Bridge
      Five Card Major Student Text 4.95
#0660 Penick-Beginning Bridge Complete 9.95
#0661 Penick-Beginning Bridge Quizzes 6.95
#3230 Lampert-Fun Way to Serious Bridge 10.00

FOR ADVANCED PLAYERS
#2250 Reese-Master Play 5.95
#1420 Klinger-Modern Losing Trick Count 14.95
#2240 Love-Bridge Squeezes Complete 7.95
#0103 Stewart-Baron-The Bridge Book 3 .... 9.95
#0740 Woolsey-Matchpoints 14.95
#0741 Woolsey-Partnership Defense 12.95
#1702 Bergen-Competitive Auctions 9.95
#0636 Lawrence-Falsecards 9.95

BIDDING — 2 OVER 1 GAME FORCE
#4750 Bruno & Hardy-Two-Over-One Game Force:
      An Introduction 9.95
#1750 Hardy-Two-Over-One Game Force 14.95
#1790 Lawrence-Workbook on the Two Over One System 11.95
#4525 Lawrence-Bidding Quizzes Book 1 .... 13.95

Prices subject to change without notice.

DEFENSE
#0520 Blackwood-Complete Book of Opening Leads 17.95
#3030 Ewen-Opening Leads 15.95
#0104 Stewart-Baron-The Bridge Book 4 .... 7.95
#0631 Lawrence-Dynamic Defense 11.95
#1200 Woolsey-Modern Defensive Signalling 4.95

FOR INTERMEDIATE PLAYERS
#2120 Kantar-Complete Defensive Bridge 20.00
#3015 Root-Commonsense Bidding 15.00
#0630 Lawrence-Card Combinations 12.95
#0102 Stewart-Baron-The Bridge Book 2 .... 9.95
#1122 Silverman-Intermediate Bridge Five
      Card Major Student Text 4.95
#0575 Lampert-The Fun Way to Advanced Bridge 11.95
#0633 Lawrence-How to Read Your Opponents' Cards 11.95
#3672 Truscott-Bid Better, Play Better 12.95
#1765 Lawrence-Judgment at Bridge 9.95

PLAY OF THE HAND
#2150 Kantar-Test your Bridge Play, Vol. 1 .... 10.00
#3675 Watson-Watson's Classic Book on
      the Play of the Hand.. 15.00
#1932 Mollo-Gardener-Card Play Technique 12.95
#3009 Root-How to Play a Bridge Hand 15.00
#1124 Silverman-Play of the Hand as
      Declarer and Defender 4.95
#2175 Truscott-Winning Declarer Play 10.00
#3803 Sydnor-Bridge Made Easy Book 3 .... 8.00

CONVENTIONS
#2115 Kantar-Bridge Conventions....................................... 10.00
#0610 Kearse-Bridge Conventions Complete 29.95
#3011 Root-Pavlicek-Modern Bridge Conventions 15.00
#0240 Championship Bridge Series (All 36) 25.95

DUPLICATE STRATEGY
#1600 Klinger-50 Winning Duplicate Tips 12.95
#2260 Sheinwold-Duplicate Bridge....................................... 4.95

FOR ALL PLAYERS
#3889 Darvas & de V. Hart-Right Through The Pack 14.95
#0790 Simon: Why You Lose at Bridge 11.95
#4850 Encyclopedia of Bridge, Official (ACBL) 39.95

DEVYN PRESS INC.

3600 Chamberlain Lane, Suite 230, Louisville, KY 40241

1-800-274-2221

CALL TOLL FREE IN THE U.S. & CANADA TO ORDER OR TO REQUEST
OUR 64 PAGE FULL COLOR CATALOG OF BRIDGE BOOKS,
SUPPLIES AND GIFTS.

Andersen THE LEBENSOHL CONVENTION COMPLETE ....$ 6.95
Baron THE BRIDGE PLAYER'S DICTIONARY $19.95
Bergen BETTER BIDDING WITH BERGEN,
    Vol. I, Uncontested Auctions $11.95
Bergen BETTER BIDDING WITH BERGEN,
    Vol. II, Competitive Auctions ....$ 9.95
Blackwood COMPLETE BOOK OF OPENING LEADS $17.95
Boeder THINKING ABOUT IMPS $12.95
Bruno-Hardy 2 OVER 1 GAME FORCE: AN INTRODUCTION ....$ 9.95
Darvas & De V. Hart RIGHT THROUGH THE PACK $14.95
Groner DUPLICATE BRIDGE DIRECTION $14.95
Hardy
    TWO-OVER-ONE GAME FORCE $14.95
    TWO-OVER-ONE GAME FORCE QUIZ BOOK $11.95
Harris BRIDGE DIRECTOR'S COMPANION (3rd Edition) $19.95
Kay COMPLETE BOOK OF DUPLICATE BRIDGE $14.95
Kearse BRIDGE CONVENTIONS COMPLETE $29.95
Kelsey THE TRICKY GAME $11.95
Lampert THE FUN WAY TO ADVANCED BRIDGE $11.95
Lawrence
    CARD COMBINATIONS $12.95
    COMPLETE BOOK ON BALANCING $11.95
    COMPLETE BOOK ON OVERCALLS $11.95
    DYNAMIC DEFENSE $11.95
    FALSECARDS ....$ 9.95
    HAND EVALUATION $11.95
    HOW TO READ YOUR OPPONENTS' CARDS $11.95
    JUDGMENT AT BRIDGE ....$ 9.95
    PARTNERSHIP UNDERSTANDINGS ....$ 5.95
    PLAY BRIDGE WITH MIKE LAWRENCE $11.95
    PLAY SWISS TEAMS WITH MIKE LAWRENCE ....$ 9.95
    WORKBOOK ON THE TWO OVER ONE SYSTEM $11.95
Lawrence & Hanson WINNING BRIDGE INTANGIBLES ....$ 4.95
Lipkin INVITATION TO ANNIHILATION ....$ 8.95
Michaels & Cohen 4-3-2-1 MANUAL ....$ 4.95
Penick BEGINNING BRIDGE COMPLETE ....$ 9.95
Penick BEGINNING BRIDGE QUIZZES ....$ 6.95
Reese & Hoffman PLAY IT AGAIN, SAM ....$ 7.95
Rosenkranz
    BRIDGE: THE BIDDER'S GAME $12.95
    TIPS FOR TOPS ....$ 9.95
    MORE TIPS FOR TOPS ....$ 9.95
    TRUMP LEADS ....$ 7.95
    OUR MAN GODFREY $10.95
Rosenkranz & Alder BID TO WIN, PLAY FOR PLEASURE $11.95
Rosenkranz & Truscott BIDDING ON TARGET $10.95
Simon
    WHY YOU LOSE AT BRIDGE $11.95
Stewart & Baron
    THE BRIDGE BOOK, Vol. 1, Beginning ....$ 9.95
    THE BRIDGE BOOK, Vol. 2, Intermediate ....$ 9.95
    THE BRIDGE BOOK, Vol. 3, Advanced ....$ 9.95
    THE BRIDGE BOOK, Vol. 4, Defense ....$ 7.95
Thomas SHERLOCK HOLMES, BRIDGE DETECTIVE ....$ 9.95
Woolsey
    MATCHPOINTS $14.95
    MODERN DEFENSIVE SIGNALLING ....$ 4.95
    PARTNERSHIP DEFENSE $12.95
World Bridge Federation APPEALS COMMITTEE DECISIONS
    from the 1994 NEC WORLD CHAMPIONSHIPS ....$ 9.95